Joseph Charless

Printer in the Western Country

Joseph Charless

Printer in the Western Country

By

David Kaser

Philadelphia
University of Pennsylvania Press

7410

Printed in the United States of America

TO MY MOTHER
who read many books

PREFACE

This book is not about a great man; on the contrary it is about a relatively unimportant man. Joseph Charless was a printer, an artisan who worked largely with his hands. He was like many of his fellows pioneers who trekked westward to people the American frontier. Except in professional matters, the adventures and misventures that befell him on his odyssey in search of permanence and security were not dissimilar from those of other craftsmen of his time who, with their families, also sought their fortunes in the Transylvania country. They contended alike with swollen rivers, Indian uprisings, and cholera epidemics. Charless' story is their story.

Even the trials in Charless' life that arose directly out of his career as a printer cannot be considered, except in accidental detail, to have been trials that he and he alone knew and wrestled with. They were trials common to every frontier printer. These men moved through the forests and plains, carrying their presses and type cases on wagons and keelboats, setting up shop wherever they were assured a handful of subscribers to their weekly newspapers. Theirs was a difficult lot. Their winter paper supply would fail to arrive from the East before ice shut off river transportation, forcing a season's shut-down and possible bankruptcy. The mail from Bardstown would miscarry so that there was no news for the weekly sheet. A postmaster of a different political persuasion would fail to forward newspapers that contained editorial matter with which he took exception. Since printers were community opinion leaders, their political tribulations took innumerable shapes. There was always the problem of tardy debtors among subscribers and advertisers, and money was scarce. In such matters as these, Charless' story is the story of other printers in the Western Country.

This little book thus becomes at once a biography of one man and a story of many men. The details are from the life of a single immigrant Irish craftsman, but the total saga is one of the great American move westward. It concerns a restless age and a migration of myriad settlers, adventurers, merchants, trappers, soldiers, and tradesmen. It is a story of the many unimportant yet capable men who created a nation out of a vast wilderness.

In preparing this story I have had aid and counsel from more people than I can ever repay. I will always owe a special debt to my quondam colleague Professor John Francis McDermott, who took time from his own researches to read an early draft of this manuscript and make many invaluable suggestions for its improvement. I am very grateful to the American Philosophical Society, which made me a grant from its Penrose Fund to offset some of the expenses incurred in doing the research. I must acknowledge with appreciation permission that has been given to me to quote from unpublished materials in the possession of the Historical Society of Pennsylvania, the Liverpool Public Library, the New-York Historical Society, the Missouri Historical Society, and the American Antiquarian Society. Librarians in three countries and in many libraries assisted me immeasurably, but the librarian who helped me most, in rendering yeoman assistance, in giving wise counsel, and sometimes just in listening sympathetically and attentively when that was what I needed most was my wife. I am grateful.

D. K.

May 29, 1962
Nashville, Tennessee

CONTENTS

LIST OF ILLUSTRATIONS

Joseph Charless

Printer in the Western Country

Chapter I

. . . OF THE CITY OF DUBLIN, PRINTER

The Irish village of Killucan stands seven miles to the east of Mullingar, capital city of County Westmeath and center of the nation's thriving cattle industry. The countryside around the village, although mostly flat, bog-stream area with woods, hedgerows, and grassy pastures, is pleasantly diversified with low hills and beautiful lakes. It is in the heart of the quiet, pastoral section of Eire's midlands that is vividly described by Maria Edgeworth and Oliver Goldsmith.

In a cottage outside the village of Killucan, on July 16, 1772, Joseph Charless was born—the same Joseph Charless who was to establish in St. Louis, Missouri, thirty-six years later the first printing press west of the Mississippi River and to begin publication of a newspaper that would flourish until 1919. He was baptized eleven days after birth and appears to have been the only child of Edward and Ann Charles, as the name was then spelled, for the parish register that records this sacrament, as well as those of his aunts, uncles, cousins, and other relatives, lists no other children to Edward and Ann.

Charles is an uncommon family name in Ireland. Although it appears much earlier, Joseph's family is reported to have been established on the island by John Charles, who came from Wales in 1663 and settled in Leinster. For a century and a half the family dwelled in and around Killucan. John's son Michael was Joseph's grandfather, and he and his wife Rachel had nine children, of whom the last, born in 1719, was Joseph's father, Edward. Although Michael and Rachel and their descendants lived in the parish throughout the eighteenth century, the name Charles is unknown in Killucan today.

The family home was the 132-acre ancestral townland of Mucklin, which in Gaelic means "pig pool," but neither the house nor the property exists today. A rath, one of the ancient, uncultivated mounds of earth traditionally inhabited by "the little people," remains inviolate opposite the house site, but otherwise Mucklin has been absorbed into the surrounding estates. Indeed the name is known today only as it refers to Mucklin Cross, a road junction near the townland of Craddenstown, three miles notheast of Killucan.

The Charles family was one of propertied artisans. Michael was a slater, and Joseph's father Edward followed in Michael's footsteps. He worked hard, however, and married well, and, before he died, could sign his name "Gentleman." Joseph's mother, nee Ann Chapman, was the granddaughter of George West of Athlone, also a gentleman. Several of Edward's brothers were men of considerable property. Brother Michael Charles was a gentleman, too; he held the townland of Grangebegg just south of Mucklin in Killucan parish. Brother Joseph Charles, Gentleman of Rossmead, held a 270-acre plantation in the half-barony of Fore in County Meath. Numerous property transactions of members of the Charles family are recorded in the deed books preserved in the Registry of Deeds, Henrietta Street, Dublin.

There are no records, however, to shed light upon the early life or education of young Joseph. He appears never to have entertained notions of being a slater, as were his father and grandfather, or, like his uncles, establishing himself as a country gentleman. When, in 1826, he announced that "he had resumed his former profession of Apothecary," [1] he was probably referring to a brief experience in that trade in 1812 rather than to any early training or apprenticeship as a druggist.

Indeed following announcement of his baptism in 1772, Joseph's name does not again appear until 1794, when he acted as administrator of his late Uncle Joseph's estate. On March 19 of that year he signed a deed "Joseph Charles of the city of Dublin Printer." [2] Some time during the preceding twenty-two years he had served his apprenticeship as a printer, and earned the rights of a journeyman.

It is not known where Joseph learned to print. In Dublin the apprenticeships of printers were usually recorded by the Corporation of Cutlers, Painters, Paperstainers, and Stationers, otherwise known as the Guild of St. Luke. Yet Joseph's name does not appear in the pages of its apprentice book,[3] which purports to include the periods of service of all apprentices in the city who worked under Protestant masters. Catholics were not at that time allowed full membership in the Guild, however, and the omission of Joseph's name from the apprentice book could be interpreted to mean that he had been articled to a Catholic printer. Or, he might have learned to print in one of the provincial towns. There was, for example, a printer named William Kidd issuing a newspaper called the *Westmeath Journal* in Mullingar as early as 1783.[4] Kidd is also known to have printed some theology books. Certainly Joseph's later work showed that he had received good training in both newspaper and book work, and he may well have learned under a master such as Kidd, but again proof is lacking.

Although Joseph was printing in Dublin in 1794, his name appears neither in the city directories of the period nor in the lists of Freemen of the city. It is not known whether he had professional association with James Charles who printed in Dublin a decade later, but the two were related by blood. James was the son of Richard Charles of Kells, a distant branch of Joseph's family, and the possibility that Joseph and James may have learned to print at the same press must be allowed.

The 1790's were troubled times for Irish printers. At no time before nor since has a government been more vigorous in its efforts to control the press. Recent revolutions in the United States and in France inspired the Irish people once again to contemplate independence from Great Britain, and it frightened the loyalist government into zealous prosecution of revolutionary thinking wherever and whenever it could be found. Printers, who had it in their power to incite the populace with inflammatory pamphlets and editorials, were carefully watched by investigators and informers from Dublin Castle. Many fled the country to escape bailiffs with warrants, and others, without benefit of legal action, simply found it desirable to flee what they felt to be government control or censorship of their presses.

Latter-day reports imply that Joseph Charless fled Ireland to avoid prosecution for rebellious activities, and such may certainly have been the case. He was a man of firm republican principles who would brook no unwarranted intervention in the freedom of his press. Yet, there appear to be no records today that would indicate that he was forced to flee his native land to escape specific legal prosecution; it is more likely that he exiled himself because he could see no satisfactory compromise between his principles and government control of his press. Some say he went first to France.[5] This may or may not be true. What is certain is that by August 27, 1795, he had established a bookstore and press in Lewistown, Pennsylvania, and was about to issue a newspaper.

Chapter II

THE EASTERN BOOKTRADE

Nothing is known of the young Joseph's adventures between the time he signed the deed in Dublin on March 19, 1794, and the writing of his first extant letter in Lewistown, Pennsylvania, on August 27, 1795, but two statements that he made later in life shed some faint light on this period. Writing in October of 1817, Charless commented that "Twenty three years ago, the editor of this paper bore arms in defence of his adopted country." [1] That would have been in the fall of 1794. There were Indian wars at that time and the Whiskey Rebellion in western Pennsylvania. Was the Irish immigrant among the conscripts sent to suppress that insurrection? Perhaps. Charless' second comment pertaining to this period reads "In the year 1795 I first visited the western waters, as low down the Ohio as the rapids, where a few stores and taverns constituted Louisville a town." [2] How long he had stayed in Kentucky or what his purpose was in visiting the Western Country in these early days is not now known.

By August, however, the printer had returned east and had settled in the village of Lewistown, in Mifflin County. Located on the Juniata River at a former Shawnee village site, Lewistown was already four decades old when

Charless arrived there. When the Pennsylvania traders
began their east-west treks over the Alleghenies, one of
the most-traveled routes was over the Juniata Path
through Lewistown, and the town prospered from the
commerce. It had been plotted in 1790 and must have
appeared to young Charless to be a likely place in which
to establish a press.

His stay in Lewistown may be sketched, but only
lightly, from a brief series of letters [3] that Charless
wrote while there to the Philadelphia printer-bookseller,
Mathew Carey. By the time he wrote the first on August
27, 1795, Charless had already obtained "a great number"
of subscribers to a newspaper, which he planned to
publish as soon as his paper supply arrived. He was in
need of an apprentice, "or if he knows Any thing of Case-
work," would employ a journeyman. And he announced
that the assortment of books sent to him by Carey ought
to sell well in Lewistown. Business prospects were good,
and he sent his regards to Mrs. Carey.

Charless wrote a second letter two months later, and
by this time his newspaper was underway, because he
enclosed a copy of one of his first numbers. No copies of
this paper nor of any other Lewistown printing by
Charless are known to exist today. Indeed, except for one
obscure reference in a contemporary document, even the
title of the newspaper would now be unknown; the
minutes of the commissioners of Mifflin County, Pennsylvania, record that on May 18, 1796, the commission ap-
proved for payment an invoice from Charless for having
advertised in his *Mifflin Gazette* proposals for building
a new court house.

Charless' letters from Lewistown are pure business
correspondence and tell very little of the booktrade in

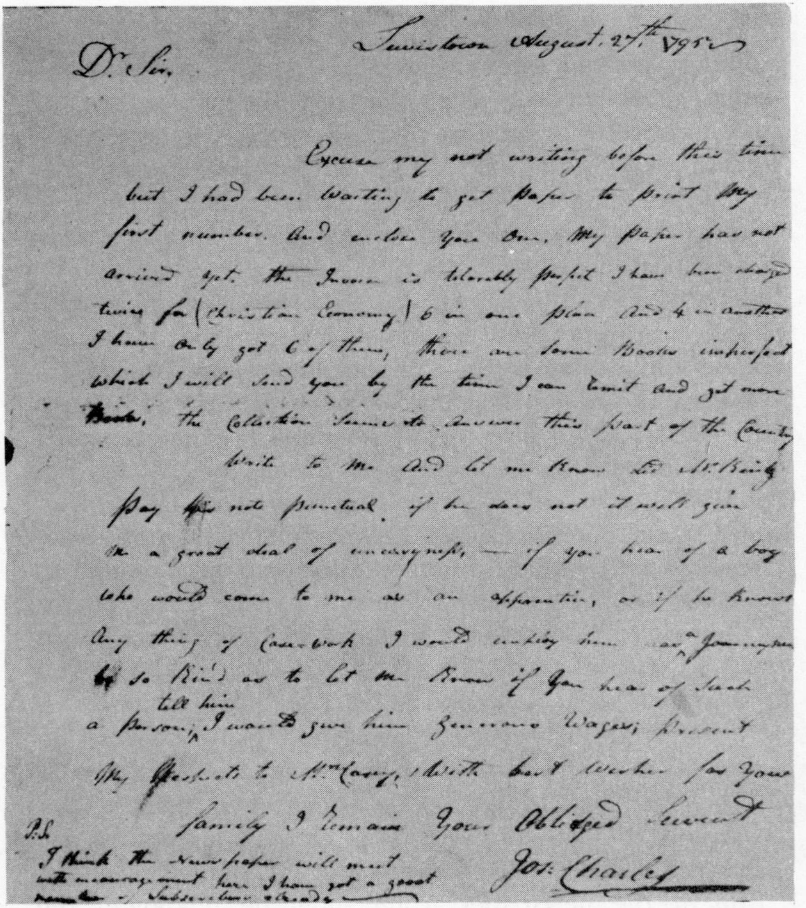

The first extant Charless letter

that place. He reported on October 27, 1795, that "I could sell a vast Quantity on credit, if I had a large store which I will endeavour to accomplish, the store-keepers here will sell no more Books, but leave me the exclusive sale of them." But he did not say what kind of books would sell. A letter enclosing. an order has been preserved, but the enclosure listing the titles he wished to purchase has not. It probably differed little, however, from the invoices of other small, country bookstores of the period and contained many religious disquisitions, school texts, medical and legal treatises, political pamphlets, hymnals, almanacs, literary works and children's books.

It is not surprising that Charless had established a relationship with Mathew Carey immediately upon his arrival in this country, because Carey himself had experienced much the same sequence of circumstances a decade earlier. Prosecuted and persecuted for operating a liberal press in his native Dublin, he had found it expedient to flee Ireland at night disguised as a woman. Arriving in Philadelphia, Carey had established a very successful book and printing enterprise that continues even today as the publishing firm of Lea & Febiger, the country's oldest house. It may have been Carey who encouraged the young immigrant to ply his trade first in a frontier village. Carey himself had early contemplated going "into the country" but after meeting a young lady and borrowing money from the Marquis de Lafayette had decided against it.[4]

The full extent of Charless' debt to Carey cannot be calculated, but certain deductions are probably warranted. That the invoice of books that Carey had sent was supplied on credit is made clear in the letters. That

Carey had helped Charless become acquainted with people in the Philadelphia trade and business community may be deduced from the comments and messages included in the letters. That Carey took Charless into his home and family is implied in the latter's recurring remembrances to Mrs. Carey. And that Carey was the early mentor in the American trade to almost every immigrant Irish printer during the half-century following his own arrival here is a matter of record, so it may be assumed to be true in Charless' case. Whether or not he lent him cash is not known, but it would not have been unusual.

It was during his stay in Lewistown that Charless first came to learn that, although Mathew Carey was a most liberal philanthropist, he was a hard creditor and, although a good business man, a poor bookkeeper.[5] Almost every bookseller who traded with the Carey firms until the retirement of Mathew's son in 1838 had to find this out for himself. Before the end of 1795 Carey was dunning Charless for a remittance—a remittance that Charless was not yet obliged to make, having had his credit on a six-month term that had not yet elapsed. Nonetheless, Carey sent abrupt notes and pressing demands for payments. On the other side, Charless was not an ideal debtor, and throughout his dealings with the Philadelphian there were incidents of late payment of debts. On one occasion Charless, hearing that beeswax sold high in Philadelphia, sent a 164-lb. cask of it to Carey in payment of an invoice. The latter much preferred cash and wrote back that Charless had "been miserably misinformed as to the price of Bees wax." [6] Cash was a scarce commodity on the frontier, however, and was difficult to ship safely, so payment in trade was not unusual.

In 1795 Joseph changed the spelling of his last name. Readers of Thackeray's novel *Pendennis* will recall that the Irish Captain Costigan's pronunciation of the given name of his son-in-law Sir Charles Mirabel is phonetically recorded as "Chorlus," which is as it should be, since in Ireland the name is uniformly pronounced as a bi-syllable. Finding that Americans did not use this pronunciation of his family name, Joseph Charles added a second "s," thus converting it into a name that defied pronunciation except as a bisyllable. His signature to the August 27, 1795, letter was his last known use of the earlier spelling, and his October 27 letter was the first use of the latter spelling, although for some time thereafter others frequently omitted the second "s" when referring to him.

The correspondence files of the Carey firms contain one brief and interesting letter written in a neat, firm hand from Lewistown on November 18, 1795. It is signed by "Letitia Charless" and reads in full:

Mr. Charless has been ill these few days past and was not able to write to you. He desired me to inclose a list of Books which he begs you will send as soon as possible. A remittance will be sent by the next opportunity.

P.S. Be so kind as to have the Books, Ready for the bearor to take with his own Goods.

Five days later Charless wrote that "I was sick a few days ago when my wife wrote to you." This is the only known reference to a Mrs. Charless during this period. Three years later Joseph married a Philadelphia widow, but his earlier wife, Letitia Charless, must remain un-identified. No marriage record for the two exists in Joseph's home parish of Killucan, and the Dublin registers are incomplete for the period. Joseph could, of course, have met and married Letitia in America, but the Philadelphia registers do not show it, and those for Lewistown no longer exist. In her brief letter she gives no indication of being personally acquainted with the Careys —her husband usually did—leading to the speculation that the two had met and married after his departure from Philadelphia, but since he could probably not have arrived in Lewistown much before midyear, that would have allowed only a brief courtship. And what happened to her? Without this single letter we would not know of Letitia at all; with it we are left with a mystery.

By March of 1796 Charless was ready to abandon his Lewistown venture. His financial condition was complicated by the fact that he had over £100 worth of books in his possession remaining unsold, and half of his newspaper subscribers had failed to pay him. He negotiated with a "Mr. Duffy of Philadelphia" who was interested in purchasing his printing office for £250.[7] Whether or not it sold on these terms is unknown, but Charless appears to have left central Pennsylvania soon thereafter.

In his last letter from Lewistown Charless wrote, "When I arrive in Dublin I hope (With the encouragement of the Booksellers of this Country) to print Books for the American Market." He then disappeared from view for a year. There is no record of his activities on either side of the Atlantic until the following year when he published a book in Philadelphia, and although it is unlikely that he returned to his native land during this period, it remains a distinct possibility. He had friends, relatives, business, and cultural ties in Ireland and may well have found it necessary to go there. Another sentence in the same letter contains two tantalizing lacunae. "Had not a circumstance occured which calls me to

[   ]" he wrote to Carey, "I would be able to pay you the whole sum in a [   ]."

At any rate he was back in Philadelphia in 1797, for it was in that year that the printer Robert Aitken [8] of No. 22 Market Street printed "for Joseph Charless" Charles Dibdin's *Museum; Being a Collection of the Newest and Most Admired Songs*. Charless is also at the time reported to have been working on Benjamin Franklin Bache's highly influential newspaper, *The Aurora*. Whether or not it is true cannot now be determined, but it is fact that Charless was a good friend of Bache's and helped him in the same year to print James Monroe's *View of the Conduct of the Executive*.[9] It is probable that Charless' connections with Bache gave rise to the obviously erroneous latter-day report that he was well acquainted with Bache's namesake, Benjamin Franklin.[10]

As was mentioned above, the fate of Joseph's first wife Letitia is unknown, but during his second stay in Philadelphia he became acquainted with a widow named Sarah Jordan McCloud. Sarah had been born on January 28, 1771, near Wilmington, Delaware, and had moved with her parents to Philadelphia to flee the Hessians at the time of the Revolution.[11] She had married John McCloud there in the Second Presbyterian Church on September 24, 1795,[12] but he had died a short time later leaving her with a son Robert. In 1798 Sarah and Joseph Charless were married, and in April of the following year she bore him a son whom they named Edward for Joseph's father. Both Edward and Robert were, as would be expected, destined to become printers.

Very few Charless imprints are extant for the period before 1800, yet it is known that he maintained an active press in back of No. 18, South Sixth Street in Philadelphia.[13] From April 13 to May 25, 1799, he printed the

Weekly Magazine there for Ezekiel Forman, but in April
of the following year he again considered going into the
country and appears actually to have established a printing office in Gettysburg, some 125 miles west of Philadelphia. On April 2, 1800, Charless had published in the
York Recorder his "Prospectus of a Weekly Advertiser;
by Joseph C. Charless," to be printed at Gettysburg. Subscription price was two dollars per year, one-half in
advance and one-half at the end of six months. Apparently his experience with dilatory subscribers to the
Mifflin Gazette had taught him to exact at least partial
payment before delivery. In accord with frontier custom,
however, payment would be accepted "in any kind of
merchantable produce." Persons who were obtaining subscribers were directed to forward their subscription lists
"to Gettysburg as soon as possible, directed to the Printing Office of the Gettysburgh [sic] Gazette." There is no
printing extant that was done on this press, nor is there
any record of any ever having actually been done. Indeed
it is unlikely that any printing was done in that place
until Robert Harper set up his press there some seven
months later and began issuing his *Centinel*, a newspaper
that continued through the Civil War.[14]

During the year 1800, Joseph Charless was also main-
taining an active press in the fraternal city. He worked
for a time in alliance with another printer named Isaac
Ralston using the style Charless & Ralston. Their joint
imprint is on at least two books, Condie's *Biographical
Memoirs of George Washington* and Dodsley's *Economy
of Human Life*. He also printed John Murdock's *Beau
Metamorphized* "for the author," and a children's book
named *Choice Tales* "for Mathew Carey." Although the
imprint on this latter title reads 1800, it was probably

not actually issued until the following year; at any rate, it is not posted in Carey's account books until February 1, 1801, when Charless is credited with $26.20 for having composed the type and an additional $24.00 for having pressed forty-eight tokens of the work. A token, among Philadelphia printers, was 250 impressions.

The Carey account books, which are preserved in the American Antiquarian Society, detail the business transactions of the two men between July 23, 1799, and November 3, 1802, but by far the majority of them took place in 1801. They have been well described by the indefatigable researcher Douglas C. McMurtrie in his article on the early career of Joseph Charless,[15] but in the interest of the continuity of the story their substance will also be reported here.

Choice Tales, mentioned above, is only one of many interesting children's books printed by Charless for Carey in 1801. Children's books were in great demand during this period, and Carey, anxious to do all he could to supply them, published many tiny volumes of banal tales replete with bad pictures. As are comic books today, these important social documents were literally read to pieces in the hands of American youth and have become rare to the collectors of juvenilia. Among the many children's books that Charless printed for Carey in 1800 and 1801 were 1250 copies of *Little Boy Found under a Hay Cock,* 1500 copies of *Many Boys and Girls,* and 2000 copies each of *Goody Two Shoes, Little Francis, Giant Grumbo,* and *Whittington and His Cat.* They, too, are recorded in Carey's account books.

Charless liked to recall in later life that he had been the printer who had composed and printed the first edition of Mathew Carey's renowned quarto and duodecimo

editions of the authorized version of the Bible. Carey had
become well known as a Bible publisher as early as 1790
when he had issued the first American edition of the
Catholic Rheims-Douay version. In the course of a few
years his firm became one of the largest and most
important Bible publishing houses in the country. It also
issued over sixty editions of the Protestant King James
version. After his success with the Douay version, it is
not surprising that Carey should have invited Charless,
in the spring of 1801, to submit proposals for the printing
of the authorized translation. Charless submitted his proposal as follows on April 15:

According to your directions I lay before you the conditions
already spoken of and agreed upon for Printing 2000 Number
of a Quarto Bible—

Suppose 120 sheets of which I engage to execute one
Sheet per day—Provided the Font is large enough to employ
a Sufficient number of Compositors, the proofs read and re-
viser examined with due expedition—

Mr. Carey allows $1000 For Types and Printing remainder
of the amount to be paid in Books & Stationary at 40 Cents
per 1000 [ems]—and 3 shillings and 6 pence per Token—
Viz—for Printing.

$40 per Week for 120 Working Days	$800.00
400 Wt of Pica Small Pica @40	160.00
50 Wt of Non P. @100	50.00
	$1010.00

Apparently these or similar terms were acceptable, because the Carey account books show a payment to

Charless dated August 1, 1801, for having printed prospectuses for the proposed Bible.

The Bible contract was certainly a very large one for
Charless and was no doubt large even for Carey. During
the time that the work was in press both men appear to
have suffered trepidation as to its financial soundness.
Both men were hot-headed Irishmen, and that tempers
sometimes waxed warm is manifest in the following letter
from Charless, dated August 11, 1801:

Dear Sir,
The expressions you made use of to me in your Store to-day
before a number of people sinks me to the earth. You told
me "I was cutting your throat" Good god Sir What do you
infer, I was so astonished I do not recolect what you said
after—if anything is going wrong I will as far as my abilities
permit rectify it. I most solemnly declare I pay every attention
to to [sic] the execution of your work. Should I do otherwise
I should be guilty of a crime I abhor, *Ingratitude—*

I am sorry to have lost your friendship I hoped to preserve
it until the Bible was finished, (if it is in my Power) let me
know how I can regain it, which will relieve Yr distressed
Joseph Charless.

The letter ends with "Forgive this incoherent scrawl."

The Bible was finished in September, by which time
any misunderstandings between the two men appear to
have been resolved. Three letters from Charless to Carey
written from New York early in that month seem to indicate that Charless had at least some of the Bible, if not
all, printed in that city. The first, which is dated September 6, announced that he had arrived in New York that
morning and was engaged in supervising, with the help

of Mr. Hugh Gaine,[16] the crating for shipment by water
to Philadelphia of both printed sheets and standing type
forms of the Bible. Gaine had had experience with this
kind of activity before. Nine years earlier, in preparation
for issuing a Bible of his own, he had imported type for
the whole work that had been set in Scotland and was
shipped to Philadelphia tied up in pages.[17] Charless wrote
again on the following day describing the special wooden
boxes he was having built in which to ship the forms and
announcing that "Mr. Gaine had obtained a careful captain to take the Boxes in Charge and every care will be
taken to put them up safe, the Sea-Flower Captain Bird
will sail positively on Saturday." An undated third letter,
probably written on the 9th or 10th—marked "Recd Oct.
[i.e., Sept.] 11"—informed Carey that "I have shipped the
Bibles, Sheets, & Mr. Gains young man will get the bill
of lading, the Loose Types will be shipped this evening,
the Vessel Sails tomorrow, I am just leaving the City."

Apparently the Bibles were satisfactory, because the
Carey account books record a credit to Charless' ledger
on September 26 of $2,278.80 itemized as follows:

To printing 2000 Copies Quarto Bible, viz:
   Composition
   98 Sheets 38000m's per Sheet, @40/
     per 1000m's   1489.60
   ⅝ of a Sheet, Sig 5G, 23750m's @40   9.60
   ½ Sheet Family Record 10000m's @40   7.60
   ⅗ Sheet preface 33600m's @40   13.20
   ½ Sheet Subscribers Names 16128m's   6.40
   Press Work
To working 100 Sheets at Press,
   16 Tokens each, at 47 per Token   752.40
                                     ———
                                2278.80

This was a very large sum in those days, reflecting the magnitude of the responsibility involved. Charless' reliability as a printer may also be noted in the fact that approximately 130 working days (assuming six per week) passed between the date of his proposal and the probable date of delivery of the Bibles. This is very near to the 120 days that his proposal estimated would be the time required. Printers are not always so prompt. The Bible was a highly profitable enterprise for Charless, and it "fully equalled [Carey's] most sanguine expectations." [18] The degree of success that the project attained from Carey's viewpoint may be assumed from the fact that he continued to issue Bibles for a quarter-century thereafter.

In addition to the extensive work that Charless did on Carey's Bible, he also printed other books in 1801. Also for Mathew Carey, he printed 750 copies of the popular 480-page legal treatise with the protracted title *Conductor Generalis, or, The Office, Duty, and Authority of Justices of the Peace, High-Sheriffs, Under-Sheriffs, Coroners, Constables, Gaolers, Jury-Men, and Overseers of the Poor: As Also, the Office of the Clerks of Assize and of the Peace &c.* For Henry and Patrick Rice, booksellers of No. 16 South Second Street in Philadelphia, he printed Corry's *Life of George Washington,* and he printed a third edition of *The Poor Gentleman* for his countryman and fellow exile, Patrick Byrne, Catholic bookseller who had been allowed to depart Dublin for Philadelphia following his arrest in 1798 for proclaiming his nationalist convictions too loudly.[19] All these books, added to the job work that Charless must have been called upon to perform, no doubt made 1801 a good year financially. But he could use the money. His family was growing. Another son, John, had been born that year.

Charless continued to work for Carey into 1802, but,

with the exception of manufacturing some school Bibles, his services to him were limited to job work. He operated presses in two locations that year: both at No. 12 Grays Alley, and on the northwest corner of Market and Fourth. During much of the time the Philadelphia printer John Welwood Scott was associated with him as a junior partner. At least three books were issued during 1802 with Charless' name listed as publisher, although he probably did his own printing of them as well. These were the *Union Primer*, Webster's *Prompter*, and Rippon's *Selection of Hymns*. He also devoted much of his attention at this time to printing books in a field new to him, namely, in the law, for it was also in 1802 that he manufactured for Patrick Byrne the early volumes of Vesey's reports of cases argued in the High Court of Chancery and of East's reports of cases argued in the Court of King's Bench.

By midyear Charless' attention had begun again to turn to the Western Country. As mentioned above, he had already visited the Kentucky frontier six years earlier and was acquainted with the way of life there. Also, he is reported to have become acquainted with several influential Kentuckians, including Henry Clay, who encouraged him to seek his future in the Transylvania country.[20] Charless had contractual commitments to Carey at this time, however, which he could not ignore. After much consideration he submitted to Carey the following undated proposal:

J.C. finds he cannot pursue his business on account of the high price of journey work and Marketing—Offers MrCarey the Materials in the Office fit to Perform his work the remainder I would take with me to the [Western] Country if Mr Carey would patronize My undertaking in Lexington

Where I have considerable Offers of encouragement. Mr Scott an Able Workman and an Honest man would would [sic] Superintent Mr Careys Work and a boy a good Pressman would be left in the Office. If Mr C. thinks favourably of the Plan, Charless will wait upon him When he is More at leasure.

Apparently Carey found these arrangements agreeable, because in early November all accounts between the two men were closed, and Charless prepared for his westward journey.

Charless' relationship to Carey, especially during the preceding two years, had been very useful in furnishing him important business contacts, in giving him extensive experience in the American trade, and in supplying him profitable work. McMurtrie summarizes Charless' business experience with Carey as follows:

The total of the statement of account to July 24, 1802, was $3724.60, or an average of not quite $165 a month for the twenty months covered by the statement. This does not include, of course, sundry items for which the printer received payment at the time, nor does it include the occasional drafts made by Charless on Carey for cash or merchandise. On the whole, it would seem that the connection had been a fairly profitable one for the printer.

The last item concerning Charless found among the Carey papers [in the American Antiquarian Society] is a receipt dated November 3, 1802, from Joseph Charless for $29.61 "in full of all Accounts." Prior to this is a series of fifteen receipts, from July 3rd to October 23rd, totaling $817. These receipts are all on printed forms in a bound receipt book used by Carey. It is quite evident that Charless could not have signed them if he had not been still in Philadelphia.[21]

Charless must have left Philadelphia immediately thereafter, however, because he is next heard from in Lexington, Kentucky, on January 11, 1803.

Chapter III

THE KENTUCKY COUNTRY

It is not known that Charless' family accompanied him on his trek westward, but since his wife was in Lexington by early spring, it may probably be assumed that the whole family traveled together. On the trip over the mountains to Pittsburgh in those days, men usually walked or rode horseback while their families and belongings were transported in wagons, of which many departed daily from Philadelphia. The distance was computed to be three hundred miles, and wagoners, who normally made it a journey of from twenty to twenty-four days, charged between five and seven dollars per hundred-weight for freight, depending upon the season. Inns were plentiful along the road, but travelers frequently camped out or slept in wagons.

The best mode of transportation from Pittsburgh down the Ohio River was aboard a flat-bottomed boat with square ends, known as an ark. Arks were commonly built about fifty feet long and up to fourteen feet wide, the latter dimension being dictated by a fifteen-foot chute in the falls of the Ohio at Louisville, through which arks often had to pass. Several families frequently joined together in the purchase of an ark, which could be had in Pittsburgh for some seventy-five dollars and which had considerable resale value downriver. Onto these arks, families, their household belongings, provisions, livestock, and other gear, were loaded for the long leg of their migration inland. The arks, which were usually covered, were managed by a steering oar and could carry up to thirty tons each.[1]

Charless no doubt found an ark ideal for his needs because he was carrying a great deal of freight. In addition to his family and household furnishings he appears to have been transporting the complete equipment for his Lexington printing office. Furthermore, he had with him a great many books. He had forwarded some $500 worth of books ahead of his party to the care of Samuel and George Trotter,[2] merchants of Lexington, to await there his arrival, but he also carried with him on the journey nearly $4000 worth of books and stationery of his own and two additional boxes of books being sent out on consignment by Mathew Carey.[3]

Charless soon found that November was not a good season to begin a westward journey, for winter was then settling upon the land making an already trying trip more difficult. His party was delayed by ice in the Ohio River and arrived in Lexington only "after a tedious passage of nine weeks" on a journey that was frequently possible in a fortnight.

Two kinds of financial disappointment made his trip even less agreeable than it would have been otherwise. The first was that his sponsors in Kentucky, who had promised to forward travel funds to him in Pittsburgh, failed to do so, and he was thrown onto his own devices. His only recourse was to break open the collections of books with which he had planned to stock his Lexington store and to dispose of many of them en route, thus financing his journey. This was very unfortunate because books drew little more in the markets of Pittsburgh than they did in Philadelphia. Altogether Charless had to peddle along the way some $800 worth of books, including law books, and pocket and quarto Bibles, some of them at six months' credit. At the end of the six months nearly $400 of the credit remained unpaid.[4]

The second financial disappointment of the journey is recorded in an advertisement in the *Kentucky Gazette*, January 11, 1803. It read:

Lost On Thursday last, between Licking river and Galbreath's tavern, A PILLOW CASE, containing TWO POCKET BOOKS & SUNDRY BANK NOTES On the banks of Baltimore and Wilmington, with some articles of Clothing, &c. TEN DOLLARS will be paid on delivery of the above articles to Mr. Charles Gallagher, Limestone, or to the subscriber in Lexington. JOSEPH CHARLESS.

There is no record of this loss ever having been recovered. Since the advertisement was continued a week later, it is at least clear that it was not recovered promptly.

Since Charless passed through Licking River on January 6, he probably arrived in Lexington on January 7 or 8. Lexington was at that time the oldest and wealthiest town in the West. Founded in 1780, it had, by the time of Charless' arrival, already grown to a point where it had some three thousand inhabitants. Streets were unpaved, and most of the houses were made of brick. There were two weekly newspapers already being printed in Lexington,[5] there were tan-yards, breweries, smiths, saddlers, coopers, spinners, weavers, butchers, ropemakers, and many merchants. Three years following

Charless' arrival there the town could boast of having 104 brick houses, 10 stone, and 187 log or frame houses, a court house, a market, four churches, a university, and a public library.[6] It was surrounded by beautiful farming country. Without question, Charless had selected well the city in which he was to exercise his skills, for Lexington was a thriving, prosperous, and promising town.

Also on January 11, 1803, Charless announced in the *Kentucky Gazette* that he had established in Lexington a new printing office and bookstore on Main Street, between the Bradfords' printing office and Captain Henry Marshall's tavern, where he proposed to sell books and to print a newspaper called the *Independent Gazetteer*. This newspaper would be "of a size nearly equal to the Philadelphia Papers at 12s. per annum." Within two and one-half months of his arrival he had allied himself in partnership with one Francis Peniston, and on March 29 the first number of the new weekly paper was issued.

The *Independent Gazetteer* was a creditable-appearing sheet, but it seems to have been at first almost entirely the work of Peniston. Although Charless owned the printing office, Peniston managed and edited the newspaper and supervised the apprentices. For this he had contracted to pay Charless $500 per year for three years [7] as rental. The partnership was a short-lived one, however, and Peniston withdrew on May 10 and departed for Bardstown where he established a newspaper of his own called the *Western American*. Charless then operated his printing office alone until August 16, when the *Gazetteer* announced that "Joseph Charless has taken into partnership in the Printing Business (only) Mr. Robert Kay; said business will in future be conducted under the style of Charless & Kay." This partnership was also short-lived, and on September 27 Charless withdrew entirely from the newspaper, leaving it to Kay. Thereafter he stayed out of the newspaper trade for four years. The *Gazetteer* collapsed six months later.

No doubt the failure of the *Gazetteer* was to a certain extent due to there already being, when Charless arrived in Lexington, a good printing office on the ground which was issuing a good, well-established newspaper. The printers were John and Daniel Bradford, and their paper was the above-mentioned *Kentucky Gazette*. John Bradford had been born the son of a printer in Virginia in 1749 and had removed to Kentucky in 1785. Two years later he had established the *Kentucke Gazette*, as it was first called. In early 1803 he turned the operation of his *Gazette* over to his son Daniel. There was also at that time a second Lexington paper, *Stewart's Kentucky Herald*, which had been established in 1795 by James H. Stewart. Later in 1803 Stewart appears to have removed his paper to Paris, Kentucky, where it continued for some time. Charless' relations with the other printers of Kentucky seem to have been cordial. When, on August 10, 1803, a number of gentlemen from Kentucky and surrounding regions gathered at Captain John Postlethwaite's to celebrate the session of Louisiana to the United States, it was Charless who proposed a toast that was drunk to John Bradford, "the first Kentucky printer." [8]

When the *Independent Gazetteer* ceased publication, Charless considered relinquishing the printing business entirely and restricting his activities to bookselling and publishing. On March 6, 1804, he announced his printing press for sale.

The subscriber [he advertised in the *Independent Gazetteer*] intending to embark as extensive as possible in the book business, offers his compleat Printing Office for sale on the following terms:

That the purchaser will execute for me, Printing to the amount of 1000 dol. annually, for three years, for which I will pay the prices given by booksellers in Philadelphia, as each work is compleated. The amount of the office will be required in hand. The types are new and well assorted. Other materials are nearly new, and in the best order.

The press appears not to have sold, however. On January 10, 1804, Charless had removed his operation "to the new brick house, next door to Mr. Leavy's store," and on June 19 he moved it again, this time "opposite to where it formerly was kept, between Messrs. Seitz and Sanders's stores." [9]

If Charless' newspaper venture in Lexington was a failure, certainly his bookselling operations were the opposite. He found the Western Country literally starved for books and concluded that his best opportunity for success lay in attempting to supply them. His was the first bookstore in Lexington,[10] and in his first letter east he speculated that "10 or 1200 Dollars worth [of books] could be disposed of in the States of Tennessee, Kentucky and Ohio," and that he could sell a hundred Bibles in a month. By February 22 he had had more ample opportunity to assess the western markets, and his report of that date to Mathew Carey is revealing and optimistic as to the prospects of the booktrade in that country. After complaining that Lexington mechants frequently found that they could buy wholesale lots of books cheaper in Baltimore than in Philadelphia, he explained what kinds of books would and would not sell:

Classics has a great sale here. I could sell since I arrived

some dozn of Virgels, Pantheons, Horrace, Ovid &c &c I had
about 30 in all which are sold Your Bibles are much wanted
here if you could send me 50 cop. they could be sold (the
course Kind) a concordance (Browns) is much sought after,
if you would join me in an Edition should be glad to print
one in Philadelphia. Religious books of almost every description are in demand Particularly new Authors . . . The following
are a list of the Books unsaleable which I brought out belonging to you, which by taking them with others to the more
Western Towns I think I may dispose of to advantage.

Octavo Bibles	Universal Spell. Book
Art of Reading	Adgate Music
Gough's Expositor	Ashes Gram.
Latin Primer	Harrisons D⁰
Dwight Geography	Buchanans Syntax

He then listed books he felt would sell, including
lectures, mathematics, medical works, philosophy, religious disquisitions, classics, and science. The heavy
emphasis on learned works is no doubt explained by a
subsequent letter stating that "the College here entirely
depend on me for Scientific Books." [11] That would be
Transylvania University, the oldest institution of higher
education west of the Alleghenies, which had moved to
Lexington from Danville in 1787.

Charless suggested to Carey that since cash was so
difficult to remit, Carey might find it desirable to print
catalogues of books available, complete with prices
affixed, which Charless could then distribute throughout
the countryside taking orders, rather than having to carry
a large stock of books on hand. Charless could then bring
the cash to Philadelphia in person once a year. Carey,
however, seems never to have taken this proposal to
heart, continuing rather to send out some of the books

that Charless ordered and some that he did not order—
especially books that were no longer salable on the
eastern seaboard. This latter practice troubled Charless
very much as it only increased his inventory and indebtedness without improving his fiscal condition. "You
mention in the course of ten days you would forward me
a Collection suitable to this market," he wrote on September 20, 1803. "I am glad they are not come on—as the
people are very whimsicall in the purchases of Books.
A book in demand this year will be a drug the next." Yet
Charless had also to complain that Carey was not sending
him the books he did need, although he probably guessed
correctly that he himself might have been partially to
blame for not having remitted payment more promptly.
"If you do not make up the orders and send them soon,"
Charless advised in the same letter, "I shall lose my credit
with the people as a Bookseller. You will say quick
remittance will cause the Books to travel post haste to
Kentucky.—Believe me when I tell you I have not been
able to collect the 1/6 of my Sales, and I am now determined to sell only by retail and for Cash (except
Books of my own Printing)."

With the large supply of books, both his own and
Carey's, which he had brought with him to Lexington,
and with the books he had forwarded earlier that had
been stored intact in the loft of Trotter's house, Charless
was able to stock a large store, which he called The
Kentucky Printing-Office & Bookstore.

There is no inventory of the books that constituted this
stock, but in the first issue of the *Independent Gazetteer*
Charless had itemized many of the books he had "on
hand." The list read as follows:

2 Sets Hume's History of England, with the
   Continuation,
2 Sets Shakespeare's Works, with Johnson's
   notes,
4 Chaptal's Chemistry,
2 Materia Medica,
75 Goldsmith's England, ⎫
50   do   Rome, ⎬ Abridged
                      ⎭
150 Scott's Lessons,
100 Sheridan's Dictionary, large and small,
150 Bibles, octavo school & pocket,
500 Testaments,
1000 Spelling Books, assorted,
2000 Primers
With a variety of Miscellaneous Books.

General merchants of the city volunteered to respect
Charless' specialty and gave assurances that they would
discontinue importing books, leaving the booktrade exclusively to him. Altogether this appeared to be a promising operation; Messrs. Trotter and Scott alone had been
selling books amounting to some $1500 annually as part
of their general merchandise.[12] By November Charless
was able to advertise that he had for sale "a greater
variety of New Books (Greek, Latin, and English) than
at any other store in the western country." [13]

When six weeks after his arrival in Lexington Charless
had written to Carey that he had leased out his press for
newspaper printing, he had also announced, "I intend to
devote my time and attention to Bookselling and Binding.
I can get here one Dollar per Quire Blank books
(common kind) there are more work here than 3 binders
could perform." It appears that he took considerable
pains to develop his binding business, and that business

appears to have been successful. Later in the year he advertised:

Record, Accompt, Common-Place, Pass, Cyphering and all other kinds of Blank Books, Bound in a superior manner, and sold on more reasonable terms than at any other regular Book-Bindery, I am enabled to execute work in the highest gilding, and most elegant devices.[14]

Charless had some difficulty at first retaining the services of a good journeyman binder, although he was offering wages of six dollars weekly plus room and board. His first binder planned to leave for the West Indies in April of 1803, and Charless sought Carey's assistance in procuring a replacement. Whether or not Carey helped is unknown, but by September Charless was ordering new supplies of gold leaf and marble paper and had one journeyman and two apprentices working just on his binding.[15]

It is not known who this binder was. In the September 27 issue of the *Independent Gazetteer* Charless said simply that his binding was being done "by a first rate workman, (from London)." Eighteen months later Charless was having his binding done by William Essex, but it is not clear that he had come from London. Essex had been binding in New York in 1798 and was either on his way to Lexington or had already arrived there by July, 1803. If he was actually there that early, however, he had a peculiar habit of not picking up his mail, because the *Kentucky Gazette* listed letters for William Essex among those unclaimed at the Lexington Post Office on July 5 and October 4, 1803, and January 3, April 3, and October 2, 1804. Since letters were only held three months before being forwarded to the dead letter

office, these listings could not have referred to the same
piece of mail. By early 1805 Essex was definitely in Lexington and was operating a shop "opposite Dr. Down-
ing's," on Main Street. No matter who the journeyman
was, the binding business was good, and Charless'
bindery appears to have kept busy working for private
citizens and public offices alike.

From the number of extant Charless imprints dated
1803, it appears that he must have leased out only the
editorship and management of his newspaper press during that period and retained unto himself all the book
and job work done in his office. At any rate, only one
among the eight books and pamphlets known to have
been issued by his shop during the year bears his imprint
jointly with that of another printer, Robert Kay. Among
these books was the 36-page *Charless' Kentucky, Tennessee, & Ohio Almanac, for the Year of Our Lord 1804:
Being Bissextile or Leap Year, and Twenty Ninth of the
Independence of the United States after 4th July. From
Creation According to the Scriptures, 5766. Fitted to the
Latitude and Longitude of the Town of Lexington, (K.)
But Will Serve without Essential Variation of the Adjacent States. Cantaining* [sic] a List of the Courts,
Officers of the General Government, Members of Congress, &c,* and astronomical calculations made by Abraham Shoemaker. Almanac publishing was a profitable
venture on the American frontier, and Charless issued
one every year thereafter through 1808, and later issued
almanacs in Missouri.

The other seven titles that Charless printed in 1803
were religious works. Four were commissioned by various
Kentucky church organizations, and two were hymnals.
One of the hymnals was particularly well adapted to the

CHARLESS'

KENTUCKY, TENNESSEE & OHIO

ALMANACK,

For the year of our LORD 1804:

Being Biffextile or Leap Year, and twenty ninth of the Independence of the United States after 4th July

From Creation according to the Scripture, 5766.

Fitted to the Latitude and Longitude of the town of LEXINGTON, (K.) but will ferve without effential variation for the adjacent ftates.

Containing a list of the Courts, Officers of the General Government, Members of Congress, &c.

———◁:※:▷———

LEXINGTON : (K.)

Printed and sold by JOSEPH CHARLESS ;

Where may be had a greater variety. of New Books *(Greek. Latin and English)* than at any other ftore in the weftern country. Record and Account Books bound to pattern : Fine and common Paper always for fale, by the Ream or Quire , and an Affortment of elegant Stationary..... All of which will be fold on fuch low terms, as will, he hopes, give him a decided preference.

Title page to Charless' Almanac for 1804

western market, having been selected by a Kentucky clergyman. By June Charless' first edition of 1250 copies of this work was already out of print, and he was preparing a new edition of 2000. The other book he printed that year was Jonathan Edwards' *Some Thoughts Concerning the Present Revival of Religion in New England,* a 412-page book that must also have sold well. On June 27 Charless asked Carey to notify the eastern booksellers that he had the work in press and announced that he had already obtained fully 1567 subscribers to it. These were very large editions for those days and, together with his bookselling and binding activities, manifest clearly the unquestionable success of Charless' first year in the bluegrass country.

Although his newspaper ceased publication in March of 1804 Charless kept his press busy by printing twelve books that year, of which all but one were religious works. That one was a 231-page "compendious system of vulgar and decimal arithmetic," known as *The American School-Master's Assistant.* It was a book calculated specifically for the western trade, having been written by Jesse Guthrie, an early Kentucky schoolmaster. Charless again printed, as he had the preceding year, the minutes of the Elkhorn association of Baptists in 2000 copies. Several of the works printed in 1804 were fairly pretentious ones for a frontier press and included Macgowen's *Infernal Conference* in 366 pages finished in early May, and a seventeenth-century work by Walter Marshall called *The Gospel-Mystery of Sanctification* in 287 pages. Also probably printed in 1804 was *The Importance of Family Religion,* known today in only two copies. The imprint in this work is blurred and was formerly read variously to be 1801 or 1802 and was con-

sequently thought to be Charless' earliest Kentucky printing. Since it is now known that he did not arrive in
Lexington until 1803 the earlier readings are no longer
acceptable.

During 1804 correspondence between Charless and
Carey was much curtailed, hinting that all may not have
been at its best between the two Irish-Americans. On
June 12 Charless submitted a complete accounting to the
Philadelphian of the books he had sold for him on $7\frac{1}{2}$
per cent commission and an inventory of Carey's books
remaining unsold. They were:

24	Large Bibles (Octavo)	$55.00
11	Latin Primmers	8.02
12	Buckannons Syntax	6.00
40	Goughs Expositor	7.76½
2	Browns Catechism	1.33
5	Dodsleys Tables	3.12½
		$81.24

Charless had remitted a total of $364.20 to Carey for
those of his books that had sold, and he still had this
$81.24 worth on hand. A subsequent letter dated Sep-
tember 25 contains a paragraph that may explain the
sudden coolness between Charless and Carey. "Your si-
lence gave me reason to think," Charless wrote, "[that
you] were offended with me. You Sir is the last person
I should wish to Offend. I consider myself under Various
Obligations to You And should be sorry you would think
me Guilty of Ingratitude. As you could not supply me
with classics, it was fair I should apply elsewhere." It
thus appears that, not only had Charless been dilatory in
his remittances, but also Carey had failed again to furnish

the books needed by Charless to fill his markets. Charless'
family, meanwhile, was continuing to grow. On January
17 Sarah had borne another son who was named Joseph
for his father.

As was mentioned above, Charless had peddled up-
ward of $800 worth of books along the route during his
journey west. Upon his arrival in Kentucky he had begun
making short trips to the countryside immediately surrounding Lexington, hawking his wares from cabin to
plantation to country merchant. There are records of his
having left books for sale on commission in Frankfort,
Danville, and Bardstown. The advantages of itinerant
bookselling must have been apparent to Charless as early
as November 7, 1803, when he informed Carey that "if
the Whole of the Books I ordered was in Pittsburgh I
would go on to Pitt. and carry them down in a Skiff,
which would afford me an Opportunity of Selling my
Almanacs in the State of Ohio." He does not, however,
seem to have considered until mid-1804 embarking ex-
tensively upon this kind of bookselling, which had been
successful in the hands of his erstwhile colleagues, the
colorful Parson Mason Locke Weems and James Pen-
noyer.[16]

On June 19, 1804, Joseph Charless advertised in the
Kentucky Gazette that he would retain

A man of good character who will engage to carry BOOKS
through this state and Ohio, for sale. He can be furnished
with a capital assortment of books and stationary, [sic] a cart,
harness, &c.-Unexceptional security will be required.

The advertisement does not say who was to have furnished the horse. Charless may have been prepared to do

so, for he owned at the time a five-year-old bay, sixteen hands high, which bore the brand IS on his shoulder. The horse disappeared five weeks later, and Charless, in the *Gazette* for July 24, offered ten dollars for its return if stolen, plus five dollars for conviction of the thief, or "a generous reward" if strayed.

There is no indication that Charless was successful in his efforts to attract an itinerant bookseller into his service in 1804, and in 1805 he decided to try book peddling himself. He spent July and August of that year driving a wagon, loaded with books, through the state of Ohio and the Indiana Territory selling volumes to individuals and leaving them with merchants on commission. Apparently this journey was successful, because immediately upon his return to Lexington he repacked his wagon with schoolbooks and set off for Nashville, 230 miles to the southwest, where he exchanged the lot for cotton.[17] Nothing is known today of any other such trips taken by Charless, but it may be seen that he was not a bookseller who sat in his shop waiting for patrons to enter; he appears rather to have actively sought out his customers.

Charless' 1805 imprints, for the most part, resembled those of 1804. He produced two almanacs in 1805: one for that year, which must have been delayed in coming off the press, and one for 1806; he printed Lorenzo Dow's farewell to Georgia, he issued an emancipation pamphlet, and he published six religious works. In addition he printed in 1805 a new kind of book for his press: an official document for the state of Ohio. At that time the official Printer to the State of Ohio was Nathaniel Willis of Chillicothe, but his presses must have been occupied, because Charless printed for him the *Journal* of the Ohio House of Representatives for the session beginning in

December of 1804. Altogether, Charless' known press work in 1805 was comprised of eleven books and pamphlets totaling some 722 pages of print.

In 1806, however, the books Charless printed are conspicuous for one important detail. With the exception of a twelve-page tract that lacks a printer's imprint, but which has been ascribed to Charless because of its similarity to his other work, none of them is religious in content. Indeed, except for the annual almanac and the above-mentioned ascription, all the known books issued thenceforward by Charless' Lexington press were school-books. On February 22 he announced in the *Kentucky Gazette* that he had just published the *Kentucky Preceptor, Containing a Number of Useful Lessons for Reading and Speaking, Compiled for the Use of Schools*, price three shillings. On April 16, he announced for sale Lenglet du Fresnoy's *Geography for Children*, price fifty cents, and on September 8, he announced, as "just published by Joseph Charless," Harrison's *English Grammar*, Murray's *English Grammar*, Webster's *Prompter*, and *The Union Primer*. If these last four works were ever actually produced over the Charless imprint, they were, as were so many other early American school books, literally read to pieces, because no copies of them are known to exist today. At the same time he also announced *The American Orator* as being in press, but this 300-page work was "a long time aborning" and did not actually appear until a full year later, it and the ubiquitous almanac comprising Charless' entire known book production for the year 1807.

In 1806 Charless contracted with its author for the western rights to the most renowned school book in the history of American education. The book was Noah

Webster's incredibly successful "blue-back" *Spelling Book*, of which it has been estimated a total of sixty-five million copies sold during the century it was in use! [18] Charless had forms of standing type of Johnson's improved edition of the work shipped out from Philadelphia, and he kept them standing, printing off editions as he needed them. By September 8, 1806, he had the book for sale for twenty-five cents, and by November 18 he had already struck off 5000 copies of the speller and was optimistic that he could dispose of in the Western Country alone over 12,000 copies annually. Webster's attorney in his negotiations with Charless was Henry Clay. Charless purchased the western rights for a certain period of time at annual payments of $200.[19] It is probable that Charless found the handling of this famous school book to be a profitable enterprise.

Mathew Carey meanwhile had apparently begun to feel that there would be little profit remaining to himself in further intercourse with Charless and had written to him on April 13, 1805, asking him to deliver to the Lexington merchants Maccoun & Tilford all Carey's Bibles and other books remaining unsold, to obtain from them a receipt, and to submit it with a complete accounting of their transactions and payment for the difference. Receiving no reply he wrote the same thing again on July 12. When he again received no reply he repeated his instructions on August 15 and a fourth time on September 5. On November 5 Charless finally reported that he had delivered the goods to Maccoun & Tilford but could not pay immediately for the books he had sold. "I would remit you for them but I really have no Money at present," he wrote; "be assured Sir I will remit as soon as possible, but for old Acquaintance sake I hope you will be lenient." Carey was not lenient, however; he was irate. "You ought not to have appropriated the proceeds of my Bibles to any purpose whatever," he complained on January 20, 1806, "but remitting me the amt as soon as it came into your possession." By May, Charless had still not paid over the amount due to Carey. "It is painful to me to observe that I think you use me very ill," Carey wrote on May 13. "I did not expect, nor had you any right, to keep me out of my money, to buy real estate, or to build." Following that letter there is no more correspondence preserved between the two men until 1812, but since they were doing business at that later date, it appears that again their affairs had been straightened out, if not amicably, at least to their mutual business satisfaction.

The money that Charless should have remitted to Carey does indeed appear to have been misappropriated, as Carey suspected, to a real estate venture, but it is impossible at this late date to reconstruct what that venture may have been. It is known that on March 1, 1806, the Trustees of the town of Lexington "hath granted and sett, and to farm let" to Joseph Charless an important piece of real property for a period of eighteen years, in consideration of which lease Charless had agreed to pay an annual rental of $80. That piece of property was comprised

of a Lott of ground in the Town of Lexington on which the Public Spring is situated and bounded as follows To Wit: Beginning on Main Street at the East corner of the Engine House thence South west to the corner thereof thence North west to the house occupied by John Bradford, thence South west to the first window in Said house thence South East

eleven feet; thence South West until opposite the lower
Corner, thence South West to Water Street, thence South
East binding thereon, twenty two feet, thence North East
thirteen poles to Main Street, thence North West eleven feet
to the Beginning.[20]

The only restriction placed upon Charless' use of this
property was that his deed should in no way affect a
privilege previously granted to the Lexington tanner and
currier, Engelhart Yeiser, of drawing water from the
public spring. This last qualification seems to imply that
Charless could, if he chose, have prevented others from
taking water from the spring. What Charless may have
planned to do with this property, including the public
spring, on the corner of Main and Water Streets, is open
to speculation, but he retained possession of it for twenty
months.

In 1805 Charless began to feel that perhaps his bookstore was sufficiently different from the stores of other
merchants that he ought not to be expected to pay taxes
upon it, and he presented a petition for tax relief to the
state legislature. The plea was taken under advisement
by the Committee on Finance of the House of Representatives, but after due consideration it resolved that Charless'
petition "praying that he be exonerated from paying a
tax on his book-store, and that the tax which he has
already paid may be refunded to him, be rejected." [21]
Not despairing, however, Charless the following year presented a similar plea to the county court of Fayette
County, and this time his efforts were rewarded when
an order was issued relieving him of his taxes for 1805
on the grounds that his bookstore did not come under
the normal category of a "mercantile store." [22] This tax

relief was no doubt most welcome by the bookseller, since it was in 1806 that his wife bore him their fifth child and first daughter, whom they named Ann for Joseph's mother.

In 1807 Charless began again to consider the prospects of newspaper publishing. He may have come to feel, as did most other frontier publishers, that it was futile to attempt to wrest any sizable portion of America's book publishing industry away from the geographical "axis" of Boston, Philadelphia, and New York. He needed a newspaper to keep his press occupied between what book and job work should come his way. Lexington, as was mentioned earlier, already had a good newspaper, and there was obviously little need at that time for another one there. Charless turned his attention to Louisville, which was then a rapidly growing community without an effective paper. Only one printer was working in Louisville at the time; it was Samuel Vail, who was issuing a weekly sheet known as *The Farmer's Library*. Early in the previous year Charless' old partner Francis Peniston had moved his *Western American* there from Bardstown, but that paper had gone out of existence several months later. Prospects for a new paper in Louisville looked good.

On October 4, 1807, therefore, "in consideration of seven shares being stock in & of the Kentucky Insurance Company," Charless signed over to William C. Worsley his lease on the Lexington town spring [23] and set out for the Falls City. On November 24 he issued there the first number of his new *Louisville Gazette*, a newspaper that he was to continue to publish for seventeen months: longer than he had ever before sustained one.

In his new location Charless also continued to sell

books. In the second issue of his paper, while begging the
indulgence of his subscribers for a few weeks until the
carrier became acquainted with their places of residence,
he itemized some of the books he could then supply from
stock. They were mostly schoolbooks and included:

American Orator	Arithmetic Tables
Kentucky Preceptor	Greek Grammar's [sic]
American do	Latin do
Geography for Children	Clark's Introduction
Schoolmaster's Assistant	Latin Vocabulary
Murray's Grammar	
Harrison's do	
Lyle's do	
Prompter	
Speling-Books	

There were also some religious books and hymnals. In
addition to the books that he kept on hand he also
ordered out specific titles from the eastern cities at the
request of his better and more influential patrons.[24]

It was at this time that Charless also considered enter-
ing into a new and totally different kind of enterprise. On
December 1, 1807, he published in his paper proposals
for opening a Coffee House. His description of the project
was as follows:

The advantages of having a place of resort to transact
business; also of transmitting in an instant any information,
and of having the perusal of the most interesting papers in
the United States, cannot fail of insuring success and
patronage.

Gentlemen in the country are informed that a book will
be kept at the bar, to receive any proposal of sales or purchase, and every exertion made to procure either.

Subscribers will have a room appropriated to their sole use, in which the News-papers will be kept; their room to be opened every day in the winter, from 9 A.M. until 9 P.M. In summer from 8 A.M. until 10 P.M.

Price of subscription, eight dollars per annum, paid quarterly. It is contemplated to keep files of at least fifty newspapers. The house to be opened on the 10st [sic] of December.

This venture seems not to have succeeded, but it is probably notable for being the first attempt to establish a stock exchange in Louisville. It also appears to have been Charless' first effort in the broad area of "entertaining" in the sense of playing the host. He was to return to this livelihood later.

Charless must not have remained favorably impressed with Louisville as a permanent home, for he did not stay there long. By the early spring of 1808 he contemplated moving even further into the interior of the country, to the Mississippi River town of St. Louis. He may even have visited there; the paucity of news and advertisements in the *Louisville Gazette* during the spring weeks suggests that the editor was away from his case at the time. By April his decision was made. He deeded over to the Lexington merchants, Maccoun & Tilford, his standing types and the copyright to Webster's *Spelling Book*,[25] but retained his Louisville printing office and newspaper. Liquidating as much as possible of his other Kentucky property but leaving his family behind, he set off for St. Louis by keelboat in June, taking with him some type and a twenty-four-year-old journeyman named Jacob Hinkle to establish there the first printing press west of the Mississippi River.

Chapter IV

THE TRANS-MISSISSIPPI WEST

Joseph Charless may have been unaware when he established his printing office in St. Louis that it was the first press in the trans-Mississippi West. There had been a need for a press in that country ever since its transfer from the French in 1804. Three years before Charless' arrival General James Wilkinson, then governor of the Missouri Territory, had sought aid from Secretary of State James Madison in the encouragement of a press in St. Louis.

We are exceedingly embarrased for the want of a Printing Press [he wrote on September 7, 1805] and our population will not support a public paper; we have two good compositors in the Territory, who have offered their services to print the Laws &c; and as we are destitute of Funds, we must implore the aid of Government; for at present no Law can be generally promulgated, before it had been sent to Kentucky, there printed and returned—Should it be consistent for the government to send forward a small Font of Types, with Paper Ink and apparatus, it would relieve our difficulties and if required, the Territory will doubtless reimburse the expense.[1]

There is no indication what Madison's response was,

but later in the same month Charless' quondam partner
Francis Peniston advertised in the *Kentucky Gazette* his
intention of publishing a newspaper at St. Louis, which
he proposed calling the *Louisiana Herald*.[2] He may have
received official encouragement to establish such a press,
but nothing came of the proposal.

In the early spring of 1808 the new territorial governor
of Missouri, Meriwether Lewis, found the lack of a press
in St. Louis as intolerable as had his predecessor, and he
contacted Charless offering him financial assistance, if he
would move his office to the newly acquired territory.
By the end of April in 1808 Charless had agreed to Governor Lewis' representations. On the 29th day of that
month the governor forwarded to the printer a bill of
exchange and bank notes totaling $195, which had been
subscribed by Missourians toward a $225 twelve-month
loan, to enable him to defray the cost of setting up a new
office in St. Louis. That letter, however, and the contents
appear to have been lost when the post rider was
drowned en route in the spring floods of the Little
Wabash River. Lewis then wrote to General William
Clark on May 29, apprising him of these developments,
and enclosing another bank draft of $100 for Charless and
requesting the general somehow .to make up the additional $125 pledge and to

Inform Mr. Charless that I have made no arrangements with
any other Printer [for] publishing the laws of the Territory,
but that if he calculates on my encouragement and support
he must come forward in person as soon as possible. The
Legislature will meet on the second Monday in June to revise
the laws of the Territory and will most probably originate
others, a printer is absolutely necessary.[3]

General Clark apparently convinced Charless that he should move quickly to St. Louis. Within four weeks of the time Governor Lewis wrote the above letter from the mouth of the Ohio, Charless was in the Missouri city distributing prospectuses for his new paper, which he called the *Missouri Gazette & Louisiana Advertiser*. Charless had printed the prospectuses prior to departing from Louisville and had ordered a new Ramage hand press to be sent out from Pennsylvania. The press was expected within a month.

Almost a half century later Charless' journeyman Jacob Hinkle made a statement to the effect that Charless did not go to St. Louis at all until late in the fall of 1808. His story bears repeating:

Mr. Charless, then in Louisville, obtained the contract for the Territorial printing, and having to be prepared for its execution by a given time, and not being able himself to leave, he engaged Mr. Jacob Hinkle, a Printer, to come here with the presses and types, in the spring of that year, on a keel-boat, in company with Gen. Clark, and commence the issue of the paper. Mr. Hinkle set up the first type and made up the first form west of the Mississippi.[4]

It is probable that Hinkle's recollection slipped on a detail here and that he and Charless both accompanied General Clark on the passage from Louisville, for it is known that Charless was definitely in Missouri before mid-year because Dr. B. G. Farrar of St. Louis dosed him there with calomel on June 27 and with castor oil on July 2.[5] Apparently travel had its hazards in those days; General Clark and Jacob Hinkle needed calomel themselves on June 23. It must be allowed as possible, however, that Hinkle might have preceded Charless across the Mississippi, although not by long. Later events, however, will show that Hinkle was none too reliable a witness.

The prospectus that Charless issued concerning his proposed *Missouri Gazette* is full of the high-blown diction of early Irish-American journalism and the abstract terminology typical of the early days of the Union. It is reproduced here in full:

PROSPECTUS

It is self evident that in every country where the rays of the press is not clouded by despotic power, that the people have arrived to the highest grade of civilization, there science holds her head erect, and bids her sons to call into action those talents which lie in a good soil inviting cultivation. The inviolation of the Press is co-existent with the liberties of the people, they live or die together, it is the vestal fire upon the preservation of which, the fate of nations depends; and the most pure hands officiating for the whole community, should be incessantly employed in keeping it alive.

It is now proposed to establish a Weekly-Paper, to be published by subscription at *St. Louis,* to be called the

MISSOURI GAZETTE,
AND LOUISIANA ADVERTISER;
BY JOSEPH CHARLESS.

For the reasons above stated, we conceive it unnecessary to offer any thing like professions to the public, but rather let the columns of the GAZETTE speak for themselves, and the print let to live or die by the character it may acquire, but its intended Patrons have a right to be acquainted with the grounds upon which their approbation is solicited.

To extinguish party animosities and foster a cordial union,

among the people on the basis of toleration and equal government. To impress upon the mind, that next to love of *God*, the love of our *Country* should be paramount in the human breast; to advocate that cause which placed Jefferson at the head of the magistracy, and in fine to infuse and keep alive those principles which the test of experience has so evidently portrayed its merits, to these ends shall the labours of the GAZETTE be directed.

No endeavours nor expence shall be spared in procuring the earliest Foreign Intelligence, which shall be impartially given, and a particular attention paid to the detail of domestic occurences, with extracts from the proceeding of the state and national legislature—To diversify scenes, we shall glean whatever shall be most instructive and amusing in the Belles Letters, with historical and Poetical extracts—men of genius are invited to send their production to the GAZETTE, which will be open for fair discussions on public subjects—it will disdain to direct its flights at smaller game—scurrility and defamation can never be admitted as auxiliaries—private character is one of the possessions of civil society, which ought to be held sacred; to follow a man into the circle of private life, would be a very unfair and licentious act;—therefore the editor will invariably exclude any and every piece which might tend to disturb our public officers, in the honest discharge of their duty, or the peaceful walk of the private citizen.

AVIS

Les anciens Habitans de la Louisiane, sont informé respectueusement par l'Imprimeur du Prospectus de la Gazette du Missouri qu'il se propose de reserver trois colomnes de son papier, pour publier en français les nouvelles localles et Etranggeres; les Loix du Territoire, et des Etats unis de L'Amerique, aussi bien que tous les Evenements qui demande publicité.

Le Prix est trois Gourdes per annum, et la GAZETTE sera distribuée une fois par Semaine.

CONDITIONS

I. The Gazette will be published once a week on a handsome Type and Paper, the day of publication will be regulated by the arrival of the Mail; during the session of Congress, should their proceedings be particularly interesting, a supplementary sheet shall be occasionally issued.

II. Terms of payment will be Three Dollars payable in advance, or Four Dollars in Country Produce. Advertisements not exceeding a square will be inserted one week for one dollar, and for every continuance Fifty Cents, those of a greater length in proportion.

III. The first Number of the Gazette, will appear as soon as possible, the Types being ready at Louisville, Ky. and the press expected in the course of a month, from Pennsylvania. The intended editor pledges his reputation, that there shall be no unnecessary delay.[6]

St. Louis had been established in 1764 and by the time of Charless' arrival had become a city of some 1400 souls, of whom 1000 were white and one fifth were Americans. The majority of the population was, of course, French, which explains the printer's willingness to publish up to three columns weekly in that language. The town was spread along the Mississippi River for about a mile and a half and had three streets running parallel to the river with several cross streets. There were still breastworks and stockades, as well as several circular stone towers twenty feet in diameter and fifteen feet high, that had been built for defense against the Indians.

There were no brick and few frame houses, most buildings being constructed of stone or hewn timbers. Some houses were built in the old French manner of setting wooden slabs or posts upright into the ground and filling them in with mud or stones; floors, when covered at all, were of timber, and windows were glass. Nonetheless, Brackenridge reported only two years later that "Every house is crowded, rents are high, and it is exceedingly difficult to procure a tenement on any terms." [7]

The Mississippi River town had in 1808 twelve mercantile stores, and the chief trade was comprised of lead, furs, and peltries. Mail was scheduled to arrive weekly from Cahokia on the Illinois side of the river, although the schedule seems at times to have been overambitious. St. Louis had already become the political and economic center for a considerable area, as well as an important military headquarters. Rustic though it may have been, it was obvious to Charless that it had a promising business future.

In this setting Charless and Hinkle obtained 174 subscribers to the *Missouri Gazette* and set up a press in the north end of a house of standing posts, known as the Robidoux house, on the east side of Main Street between Elm and Myrtle, near the corner of the old market. This was in the center of the tiny business district, which extended along Main Street from Pine to Spruce. Hinkle, his wife, and child are reported to have lived in the other room of the two-room Robidoux House.

The popularly received tradition that the press set up in Charless' new printing office had been built by Alan Ramage has in recent years been challenged[8] by reference to a statement published on December 10, 1877, in the *Missouri Republican*, lineal descendant of the *Missouri Gazette*. This statement was based upon the reminiscences of George Knapp, who had begun working with the *Republican* in 1827 and had later become one of its proprietors. Although Knapp recalled that the original Charless press had been discarded before his apprenticeship there began, it was his impression that it had been "a primitive machine, of Western manufacture," whereas Ramage presses had been built in Philadelphia. Whether or not the first Charless press was "of Western manufacture," it was definitely a "primitive machine" by modern standards. Adam Ramage had come from Scotland to Philadelphia where he had begun building presses of Honduras mahogany "with ample substance and a good finish, which gave them a better appearance than foreign made presses, and they were less liable to warp." As a result of Ramage's work, the importation of presses from abroad had practically ceased by 1800. By the time Charless ordered his press, Ramage had also greatly improved the screw and other parts connected with it by altering the ratio between the diameter and fall of the screw, thus giving it more power than earlier presses.[9] It is doubtful, furthermore, that there were in 1808 any presses of western manufacture capable of accomplishing Charless' work.

At any rate, on July 12, 1808, the first newspaper printed in the trans-Mississippi country was taken from the forms of the new St. Louis press and distributed to its subscribers. It was a very small folio sheet with three columns to the page, each of the four pages being only 8¼ x 12½ inches in size. On the masthead was the rubric "St. Louis, Louisiana. Printed by Joseph Charless, Printer to the Territory."

No copies of the first two issues of the *Missouri Gazette* have been preserved, but Volume I, Number 3, dated

A Ramage hand press similar to
Charless' first trans-Mississippi press

Tuesday, July 26, 1808, is still extant and has been many times reprinted.[10] All the first page of this number was occupied by an extract from a letter "upon the subject of Sir John Duckworth's late cruize" in pursuit of the French fleet in the Atlantic, written by an officer of his squadron. The second page was comprised of intelligences from Paris, Boston, Baltimore, Norfolk, Philadelphia, and Europe, received "By Last Mail." Page three contained several scraps of local news, including announcement of the conviction of two Iowa Indians for murder of a white man, a note on the impending war between the Osages and "Delewars, Shawanee's, Kickapoos, &c. &c . . . & as the Osages & Panies fight on horse back, there is no doubt of a warm and important campaign," and the results of the election of trustees of the town of St. Louis. Also on page three was printed a highly colorful sequence of twenty toasts drunk at an Independence Day banquet held three weeks earlier in Harrison, Indiana Territory, where "the utmost hilarity and urbanity, as well as harmony and order prevailed." The fourth page contained April news from London and Harwich, as well as "A List of Letters remaining in the Post-Office at St. Louis."

Altogether the first extant issue of the *Gazette* contained four advertisements: one announcing "Cash Given for Bills of Exchange on the Government" by Wilkinson & Price, one by Jeremiah Connor announcing an auction of the "Best Cogniac Brandy, that has been more than three years in Cellar in this town, Dry Goods, consisting of Cloths, Strouds, Chints's, Callicoes, Muslins, Irish Linen, Saddlery, Chewing Tobacco, &c. &c. And a large quantity of well assorted Castings and Hardware," and two advertisements by Joseph Charless himself: one for the printing of blank books, and one announcing "a Variety of School Books for sale, at this office," indicating that he planned to continue bookselling in his new location.

One especially interesting item in this issue of the *Gazette* was a note stating that "Mr. Samuel Solomon will receive subscriptions and advertisements for this Gazette, during the Editors absence to Kentucky." Charless had not disposed of his Kentucky printing office before coming to St. Louis, and pressing business now called for his return there. It is not known just when he left for Louisville, but it could not have been before July 20, because Charless on that day sat as a juryman at the special court of Oyer and Terminer in St. Louis that tried the two Iowa Indians mentioned above,[11] and it was probably not before July 22, when a check for $500 was drawn in his favor by the territorial governor.[12] He did leave for Kentucky about this time, however, and was not to return for almost four months. Jacob Hinkle was to operate the press in his absence, although Samuel Soloman would handle the finances.

Hinkle's problems in issuing the early numbers of the fledgling *Gazette* during Charless' absence were many and trying. Not his smallest problem was the uncertainty of mail delivery, a difficulty that was to plague St. Louis editors for more than a decade. On August 4 Hinkle apologized for "the barroness [sic] of the Missouri Gazette, this week, as the mail due on Sunday did not arrive." The subsequent week he editorialized briefly upon the harm done by poor mail service "to the inhabitants of this Territory since the establishment of a Gazette at the town of St. Louis it being impossible for the printer to give to his patrons early and correct accounts, either of foreign or domestic news." On August

31 Hinkle repeated his apology from August 4: the mail had again failed to arrive. By September 14 he could announce that exchanges of papers had now been established with "Printers in different parts of the Union," thus making a wider variety of news available to the printer. Also he pledged that the subsequent issue would be enlarged and would thereafter "appear in as handsome a form, and as well stored with 'the passing tidings of the times,' as his utmost care and unremitted attention can make it." Ironically, there was no paper issued the following week owing to the illness of the editor, although the issue for September 28 was indeed somewhat enlarged as promised. Similar difficulties dogged him through October and half of November.

By November 16 Charless had returned from Kentucky, where his wife Sarah had recently borne him another daughter, their last child, whom they named Eliza. He had still not disposed of his Louisville press, however, but rather continued to operate it *in absentia*. At least until April of 1809 the *Louisville Gazette* bore inscribed upon its masthead, "Printed by Joseph Charless, Main Street, Louisville (K.)," although for many months it carried a regular advertisement for the *Missouri Gazette*.

Those who wish to subscribe to the MISSOURI GAZETTE, [it read] are respectively [sic] informed that a subscription book is open at this Office. A capable Editor is employed, and a number of Gentlemen have volunteered to devote their leasure [sic] hours in writing on such subjects as will enrich its columns. Essays on indian antiquity, Mines, Minerals, and an account of the Fur-trade, with Topographical Scetches [sic] will be diligently sought after.[13]

When Charless returned to St. Louis from Kentucky in

November he was most displeased with the work Hinkle had been doing. He apologized to his subscribers for the slovenly and irregular manner in which the *Gazette* had been managed during his absence, as well as for its continued diminutive size, and assured them that if they would be indulgent a bit longer and not at that time withdraw their support he would soon issue a paper that would merit their unanimous approbation. Within a week of Charless' return his dissatisfaction with Hinkle had become more than the latter could bear, and he left. Charless, in the next *Gazette*, vented his feelings against his erstwhile journeyman in a most entertaining, although condemnatory column.

Caution ! ! ! The Printers in the United States, & the public in general, are hereby cautioned against employing or dealing with a certain JACOB HINKLE, who left this place on Monday night last, in a clandestine manner, leaving his debts unpaid to the amount of $600. The subscriber employed this speculating *genius* in Kentucky to assist him in his office in St. Louis, and advanced him to the amount of $200 in goods, &c. on account of his extreme indigence, and a desire to relieve his family: this and many other favours he has returned with *his usual* gratitude.

Information has been lately received that almost every town and village between Staunton, in Virginia, and Louisville, Kentucky, has felt the effects of his cunning sagacity in *gambling,* purchasing horses and watches, and issuing proposals for publishing *news-papers,* collecting subscriptions in advance, & then leaving his credulous subscribers without other than the mortifying *news* of his having absconded with their money. His mode is to buy horses, watches, &c. to a considerable amount, give his note at 6 or 9 months after date, sell them immediately for cash, at half cost, and give his creditors *leg-bail* for payment, even before his notes become due.

This hopeful *Sprig* is about 24 years old, 5 feet 9 or 10 inches high; he shuffles as he walks, has a shallow [sic] complexion, black and curled hair, is cross eyed, and very near sighted; in short, Dame Nature never formed his countenance to *deceive,* [tho' sad experience proves that he has outwitted even her in that respect] for she plainly stamped *The Villain* in every lineament thereof.

Since Charless is not known to have any other employees working in his St. Louis office, he may have found it necessary to operate his press alone for a time thereafter. He did not, however, advertise for a new journeyman until the following January, a thing he would most likely have done immediately upon Hinkle's defalcation, if the office had been short-handed at that time. It is, of course, possible that he had brought another printer from Kentucky with him, or he might have employed one of the unidentified compositors whom General Wilkinson is quoted above as having said were residing in the Territory three years earlier, but there is no record of either. Part of Charless' responsibility as Printer to the Territory, however, was to print the territorial laws, and he had them in press at this time. It is unlikely that he could edit and print a newspaper, make progress publishing a substantial book, sell books and stationery, and do such other job work as Charless was no doubt called upon from time to time to do, without some assistance from others, but it is not known who those others may have been.

Not only did Joseph Charless establish the first press and print the first newspaper west of the Mississippi River, but he also printed there the first book.[14] That first trans-Mississippi imprint was long thought to be [15]

The Laws of the Territory of Louisiana. Comprising All Those Which Are Now Actually in Force Within the Same. Published by Authority. St. Louis [L] Printed by Joseph Charless, Printer to the Territory, 1808. 376, [58] p. 13 x 20.5 cm.

It may now be seen, however, that this book was not published in 1808 as its imprint indicates, but rather in May, 1809, and, contrary to generally held opinion, was not the first book to appear west of the Mississippi, but was at best the second and possibly the third.

Charless was supposed to begin publication of the territorial laws immediately upon his first arrival in St. Louis, and he probably did so, although his dissatisfaction with Hinkle may have been due in part to the latter's failure to move ahead with the task. An early entry in the account book of the territorial governor, Meriwether Lewis, is dated July 22, 1808, and records an order on the Secretary of State in favor of Charless in the amount of $500.00, "it being an advance to said Charless for furnishing paper and publishing the laws of the territory 250 copies in English & 100 in French." That Charless was hard at work on the book is later manifested by his explanation in the *Gazette* of November 16 that work on the *Laws* hampered his work on the newspaper. "So soon as the Laws of the Territory are printed," he promised his subscribers, "he [the editor] will issue the Gazette on a full sized royal sheet, and trusts that his exertions will render it equal in appearance and utility to any paper in the Western Country." At this time the *Gazette* was being printed on a foolscap sheet folio.

Having begun the work in July, Charless was optimistic

that he could finish it before the end of the year. The title page, which bears the date 1808, is signature [A 1ʳ], and there being no other preliminary matter, the first law begins on signature A 2ʳ. This indicates that since the first sheet contains an integral part of the text as well as the imprint date, the title page must have been set first rather than, as was more often done, last. Since a small frontier printing office could hardly have possessed enough type to keep much of a work standing any longer than was absolutely necessary, the impressions were probably worked off as soon after composition as possible.

Charless was oversanguine, however, in his plans to complete the book in 1808. In the *Gazette* of January 4, 1809, the editor reminded readers of his promise to increase the size of the paper "as soon as the laws of this territory were printed," implying that work on the book still stood in the way of its fulfillment. On March 29, 1809, he again promised that "in a few weeks it [the *Gazette*] will appear on a large sheet."

The *Laws of the Territory* must have made its belated appearance in May of 1809. The issue of the *Gazette* for April 26 of that year is on a foolscap sheet, and that for May 24, the next extant issue, is at last on the much-promised larger paper, not quite a royal sheet, but a full-sized demy sheet folio. Also pointing to a date of publication sometime in May is the certificate printed on page 373 of the *Laws*, signed by the Secretary of Louisiana, attesting that the foregoing printed text was "compared and found literally conformable with the originals." This certificate is dated April 29, 1809, and, as did the title page, shares a gathering with an integral part of the text, proving that it could not have been added later. Further evidence that the work was finished in May is another entry in the Meriwether Lewis account book, this one date May 5, 1809. It records an additional payment to Charless of $822.00 "For printing the laws of the Territory Genl Orders Blanks for the returns of Militia &c &c" implying that the tasks were by that time completed.[16]

If the *Laws* appeared then in May, 1809, another work had preceded it. On December 14 and 21, 1808, the *Gazette* advertised as being "For Sale at This Office, An Act regulating the fiscal concerns of the Territory, defining the duties of certain officers concerned therewith, and for other purposes." This would in fact be a preprint of pages 349 to 371 of the *Laws of the Territory.* Unfortunately, no copies of this separately published act are known to exist today. Owners of the preprint probably had no need to retain copies when the act was republished in the complete *Laws* five months later. It was probably for the separate publication of this act that the Lewis account book records under the date December 28, 1808, a payment to Charless of $88.75 "for printing certain laws of the territory necessary for immediate distribution." There are no other separately issued acts advertised in the *Gazette,* and it is consequently probable that this act was the first book published west of the Mississippi.

Although it cannot now be proved, it seems reasonable that yet another booklet may have preceded the *Laws* from Charless' press. Frederick Bates, Secretary of Louisiana, delivered an oration before St. Louis Masonic Lodge No. 111 on November 9, 1808, and the Lodge, of which Charless was a member, resolved that the oration be printed. It exists today in two known copies bearing the imprint date 1809. It may be asked whether Charless found it necessary to defer printing for his brethren this nineteen-page oration for six months until the *Laws* were completed, or if he might not have found time to complete it earlier in the year 1809, in which case it would have been the second trans-Mississippi imprint.

If Charless ever did print the laws of the Territory in French, as the Lewis account book indicates he had been commissioned to do, no copy or other record of the work seems to have survived. It is known from his prospectus to the *Gazette* that Charless had a complete font of type with requisite accent marks, and he frequently printed French advertisements and announcements in the *Gazette*, although in no issue did he ever print three columns of French text as he had indicated he would. Charless at first made considerable effort to employ his French types but had little success. In the *Gazette* of December 21, 1809, he proposed publishing in French a weekly newspaper to be named *La Mouche du Ouest*, but his proposal appears to have elicited little support from the community. Three months later on March 29, 1810, he proposed publication of a *Gazette de la Louisiane* if one hundred people would subscribe, but this project also appears to have come to naught. These attempts to establish an active French press in late 1809 and 1810 could mean that his French types were then available for use following their having been tied up on some major project, such as a French edition of the territorial laws, but there is no positive evidence of such a work ever having actually appeared. In the fall of 1810 Charless advertised as follows: "On a besoin d'un jeune homme française pour apprenti dans cet office, un de la campagne sera préferé," [17] but the only sustained piece of French printing ever known to have been done on his press was a 26-page *Constitution de l'état du Missouri,* which was to be issued a full decade later. It is interesting to speculate as to why, if Charless had no more French work than he seemed to have, he would need a French apprentice at all, let alone a young man "de la campagne."

As indicated in the advertisement in his Louisville paper, Charless sought, during the early years of the *Missouri Gazette,* to make it an organ of the people, a forum for discussions of all kinds, and he frequently invited local citizens to supply material for its columns.

I beg leave [he wrote on January 4, 1809] to request those gentlemen who promised literary aid, to collect such materials as may enrich its columns and render the Gazette worthy of general request.

Essays on morals and government, concise pieces on history (particularly the early settlement and progressive growth of Louisiana,) Antiquities, Topography, Botony [sic], and vegetable Materia Medica, and Miniralogy [sic], with such hints on husbandry as may tend to induce the Planter to embrace those wonderful advantages nature has thrown in his way. Indian manners and customs with their best speeches, Cases argued and determined in our Courts, or anything that may contribute to enliven the passing moment by an ingenious Tale or Song, will be gratefully received and carefully inserted.

Throughout the early years of the *Gazette* Charless did publish a widely various repertory of material supplied by readers. On December 12, 1810, he printed portions of Marshall's *History of Kentucky.* On several occasions he printed poetry by local bards. On December 12, 1810, he printed a bit of Indian eloquence supplied by Frederick Bates, in the form of "a talk of the Big Soldier

delivered May 1807 in a council held with the Osages
by Major Peter Chouteau." [18] Early in 1812 he published
a series of articles on agriculture and animal husbandry.
In April of 1814 his columns contained, with apologies
for its "desultory style," a biographical sketch, which
purports to have been written by Charless himself, of
Mathew Elliott, England's Indian Agent for Upper
Canada. This biographical sketch was probably a chapter
from a book that he had, in an announcement in the
Gazette on the first day of the year, proposed writing
and publishing, being *A Narrative of the Indian War in
the West and the South*. Nothing more seems to have
been done on this work.

Charless also lent his columns to the printing of other
varia. On August 2, 1808, he published an Independence
Day address by John G. Heth, Esq. On January 18, 1809,
he printed "An Address to the People of America," by
John Coppinger. On the 14th of February, 1811, he published a review of *Travels on an Inland Voyage* by
Christian Schultz, a New Yorker who had visited St.
Louis the winter prior to Charless' arrival there. Four
weeks later he published an extract from *A Sermon on
Tale-Bearing* by the celebrated Scotch-American author
and jurist, Hugh Henry Brackenridge.

Without question the single most important piece of
miscellany printed by Charless in the columns of his
Gazette, however, was by H. H. Brackenridge's son, who
was also to become renowned as an author and jurist,
Henry Marie Brackenridge. It was in the *Missouri Gazette* in 1811 that the young Brackenridge first published
his series of sketches of the territory. This sequence of
articles was subsequently issued and reissued in book
form, with some alterations, as his well-known *Views of*

Louisiana. It was clear from the beginning that these essays constituted an important contribution. On June 20, 1811, the St. Louis attorney Richard Wash sent a complete file of the issues of the *Missouri Gazette* containing these essays to President Thomas Jefferson for his perusal,[19] reportedly at the President's request.[20]

Throughout his entire editorial career, of course, Charless published letters and communications in his columns. Some of these letters were signed, and some were unsigned. The latter gave rise to frequent rumors in St. Louis that the editor wrote his own anonymous communications, a speculation that may on occasion have been true.

Local news, in the modern sense of that phrase, played a very minor role in the *Gazette,* or for that matter in any other frontier paper. As McMurtrie has pointed out,

It was characteristic of the journalism of his time that local news, the events and activities of the community in which the paper was printed, were given practically no attention what ever. Now and then an item concerning some local happening, printed in the smallest type, was crowded in an inconspicuous space. But the doings of Napoleon and of the European courts filled the paper—whenever the mail arrived with the eastern exchanges. To make material of the interests that concerned the people of St. Louis in their day-to-day work would have been "to follow a man into the circle of private life," which according to the principles set up by Charless in his prospectus, "would be a very unfair and licentious act." With a wealth of material all about him, the editor of a hundred years and more ago deplored the lack of news and bored his readers with "fillers." Charless was no exception to the prevailing rule.[21]

Notwithstanding his disinclination to report the local

news, Charless' printing office became the information center of the frontier town. Since he received newspapers on exchange from all the major publishers in the east, his office soon became the reading room for merchants, lawyers, trappers, mountainmen, keelboatmen, and Indians, soldiers and politicians. Here they gathered to sift intelligences from the rest of the nation. The Scots naturalist John Bradbury tells of visiting an Omaha village over five hundred miles north and west of St. Louis in 1810, where two Indians indicated to him that they had seen him before.

I had no recollection of these Indians, [he wrote] but they pointed down the river to St. Louis: afterwards they took up the corner of the buffalo robe, held it before their faces, and turned it over as a man does a newspaper in reading it. This action will be explained by relating that I frequented the printing-office of Mr. Joseph Charless, when at St. Louis, to read the papers from the United States, when it often happened that the Indians at that place on business came into the office and sat down. Mr. Charless, out of pleasantry, would hand to each a newspaper, which, out of respect for the custom of the whites, they examined with as much attention as if they could read it, turning it over at the same time that they saw me turn that with which I was engaged.[22]

Charless and Bradbury became well acquainted during the latter's visit to the Western Country in 1809 through 1811. Indeed it appears that the Scot sought Charless' assistance in obtaining an English publisher for some of his writings. On December 22, 1811, two and a half weeks after Bradbury's departure from St. Louis, Charless had written to the wealthy Liverpool business man and historian, William Roscoe, to determine if he would sponsor such a publication. The letter read as follows:

Sir,

I have taken the liberty to transmit to your patronage a work I wish to have published in England entitled Sketches of Louisiana &c. Since Mr. Bradbury wrote the enclosed I have collected an appendix which I hope will be found interesting. The facts stated, can be depended upon, as well as the indian speeches. If they should be considered of any Value I would be very glad to receive Printing Type for the *compilation*. with extreme reluctance I have been urged to this step and hope you will not consider it an impertinant intrusion—Cut off as I am from procuring a supply of Types (my letter in use, being nearly worn out) I beg you to attribute my necessities as urging me to the measure.

In the Box which conveys the Sketches, I have sent [a] few articles of Indian Costume &c. and shall trans[mit] some other articles in the spring, which I beg you [to ac]cept. I would transmit my Gazette to Mr. Mr. [sic] Kenner [in New] Orleans (to whose care I consigned the Box) if you should [be]lieve them worth forwarding to you.

I am Sir,

Your very Obed. Servant

Joseph Charless

P.S.   Last Monday morning we had five shocks of Earth Quake, the first commenced at 20 Minutes two & the the last at about 8 o'Clock—I will enclose you the particulars.

J. C.

Contents of the Box sent to Messrs. Kenner & Co. New Orleans, for Wm. Roscoe Esq.

> A Calumet, or peace pipe from the Arikara
>   Indians
> One Bow & 12 arrows used by the Sieux Indians
> Dress Shirt of the Calve Skin
> Breech & leggins of fawn Skin
> Summer robe, Buffaloe calf   } Costume of the
> Winter robe, Buffaloe Bull-with the } Mandan Indians
>   exploits of the owner painted
>   thereon

7. Mokasons, or Indian shoes
8. Otter Skin Medicine bag, worked with porcupine
quills from the Sieux indians.
9. Indian cap Fox Skin—
10. Bowl of a pipe dug out at Fort Belle Fountain
on the [   ].
11. Petrified Buffaloe horn, found on the shore of the
Missouri
12. Specimen of ancient indian pottery—Louisiana
m[   ].[23]

It is not known that Roscoe obtained a publisher for
Bradbury's book, but it was published in Liverpool for the
author some six years later. It was successful and went
through two editions in two years.

Chapter V

A FRONTIER EDITOR

During his first six years in St. Louis Charless found many difficulties standing in the way of the successful operation of his press. Even as it had troubled Jacob Hinkle, poor mail service continued to plague the proprietor. On one occasion in the winter of 1808-1809 no mail arrived in St. Louis for fully nine weeks, and the editor finally had to employ a special messenger to go to Vincennes, 150 miles to the east in the Indiana Territory, to fetch it and to learn the occasion of the delay.[1] The messenger returned in less than two weeks, however, with only a handful of letters and newspapers, the most recent of which were fully three months old, indicating that the delay must have, in part, been still further to the east. Once, in September of 1809, the post rider arrived in St. Louis having lost part of the mail, and in April of 1810 the mail was delayed for two weeks because the flies were too thick in the woods and water-courses.[2] On at least one occasion Charless complained directly to the Postmaster General.[3]

The post office ought not, however, to be here deprived of some defense. Mail on the frontier was delivered by a local person under contract to the U.S. Postmaster General, and Washington, D.C. being so far distant, the government was frequently able to exert only limited influence over its local handling. There was always the danger of Indian attack, or of flood, and passage in winter was sometimes so difficult as to require fully six hours to drag a sled load of mail as short a distance as five miles. Furthermore, routes were laid out so as to pass through as many towns as possible, with no reference to topography, and as a result the carrier was frequently forced to traverse very difficult terrain.[4] Charless and other St. Louis editors had to contend with poor mail service well into the period of Missouri's statehood in the 1820's.

Not the least of a printer's problems in the early days of the frontier was the availability or unavailability of adequate materials for printing, especially of paper. Charless too faced this difficulty. It is said that the first paper used by him on the *Missouri Gazette* was of local manufacture,[5] but within six months he was desirous of using eastern paper, and in February of 1809 he ordered a supply from Pennsylvania. It was slow in coming, however, and when his old supply was exhausted at the end of March he was forced to print the *Gazette* four columns wide on both sides of a broad sheet of writing paper. Charless continued to use writing paper until late in May, when the newspaper at last appeared on full-sized paper. The paper used during the early period of the *Gazette*'s existence was manufactured by the Jackson & Sharpless mill, which was located on Redstone Creek, near Brownsville in western Pennsylvania.

The War of 1812 was especially hard on Charless because supply lines to the east were subject to attack by the enemy and were consequently infrequently traveled. Not only was his mail delayed but he also ran out of ink in mid-1812 and had to make shift for several months.[6]

Missouri Gazette.

VOL. I.   TUESDAY, JULY 26, 1808.   No. 3.

ST. LOUIS, LOUISIANA,
PRINTED BY JOSEPH CHARLESS,
Printer to the Territory.

---o---

Terms of Subscription for the
MISSOURI GAZETTE.

Three Dollars paid in advance.

Advertisements not exceeding a square, will be inserted one week for one dollar, and Fifty cents for every continuance, those of a greater length in proportion.

Advertisements sent to this Office, without specifying the time they are to be inserted, will be continued until forbid, and charged accordingly.

---o---

LONDON, April 22.

Upon the subject of Sir John Duckworth's late cruise, we have been favored with the following extract of a letter from an officer belonging to the squadron, dated

"Casand Bay, April 18.

"Having run down the Bay of Biscay, and called off Capes Ortugal and Finisterre, and Lisbon, we arrived off Madeira, and found Sir Samuel Hood, laying in Funschall roads, where we remained for two days. On the morning of the 3d of February, his majesty's ship Comus, gave us intelligence of her having been chased two days before to the N. W. of Madeira, and it then became obvious that the destination of the French squadron was the West Indies, for which we proceeded with all the expedition & made the islands of St.Lucia and Martinique in twenty one days. Off the east end of Martinique we saw six sail of the line; we cleared for action, and formed the line of battle, but, on exchanging signals we found instead of enemies; it was Sir Alexander Cochrane, with his squadron, who was waiting to give that enemy a reception which we were in chase of, conceiving that he would take refuge in that port. Finding that his fleet was sufficient to cope with them in those seas, we passed all the Windward Island, and anchored on the 16th of February in Bassaterre Roads, St. Kitts, where we remained only 18 hours, just long enough to take in water, but no provisions, nor even linen washed. We then proceeded to Saint Domingo, where it was supposed the enemy had proceeded for the purpose of landing troops; but on our arrival there we found no ships. After cruising in the Mono Passage for seven or eight days, we made all dispatch for the coast of America, and arrived off the Chesepeake on the 11th March. We communicated with the Statira frigate, and found that our Ambassador, Mr. Rose, was at Washington for the last time, to determine whether it should be peace or war with England. We should have gone in, but the Yankies would not let us have a pilot, nor supply us with water and provisions, which forced us to be content to live upon half our usual allowance ; they would not give us a single pint of water or a cabbage stock. We left the Eurydice, to bring us any intelligence that might occur as to peace or war with America, and quitted the inhospitable shores of America for the Western Islands, where we procured all we wanted, after a long and very anxious cruise. The Governor of Flores [a Portuguese,] came off to us, but not being able to give us any information, the Admiral thought it most expedient to proceed for England, where we arrived this morning, after having been three months at sea, and made a complete circuit of the Westesn and Atlantic Ocean, a journey of upwards of thirteen thousand miles."

We learn by other letters, that our squadron remained several days off the Chesepeake, and that the treatment it experienced was such as by no means to encourage the hopes of late entertained by many, of an amicably termination of our present negotiation with the United States. It is certain, that no article whatever of supply could be obtained by our admiral from the inhospitable and hostile Amerians ; and it follows of course, that the reparation offered by our government for the affair of the Chesepeske frigate was made in vain ; although that circumstance alone, since so amply atoned for, was assigned by the President's proclamation as the motive for prohibiting all intercourse between the inhabitants and such British ships of war as might arrive in the American waters. Such conduct argues so hostile a determination to the government of the United States, that the general opinion expressed by the officers of our squadron, "that a war with America is inevitable," cannot be considered as founded upon weak or trivial, grounds. We should have expected that Mr. Rose's mission would at least have procured for our squadron the rights of hospitality, if it did not effect a complete re-establishment of the former good understanding between the two countries; but we fear the Frenchified government of the United States has so far resigned itself to the baseful influence of the cabinet of the Thuilleries, that nothing but salutary chastisement will bring it to a due sense of the pernicious error into which its unnatural propensities have permitted it to be led. If America will have war with Great Britain, she will have herself only to blame for the consequences. It is our sincere wish to remain at peace with her, and our ministers, it is well known, have adopted every expedient short of comprising the honor, the dignity of the nation to avoid the extremity of warfare; but we are certainly not prepared to lay the honor and essential interests of the empire at the feet of any junto upon earth. The blustering American demagogues may perhaps have founded some portion of their confidence upon the support of a certain party in this country; some of them, as we lately took occasion to remark, may derive hope from the confiscation of property and the non-payment of debts ; they may conceal from themselves their comparative impotence, by throwing their weight into the aggregate of the enemies of G. Britain; but a few short months of war would convince these politicons of the folly of measuring their puny strength with the colossal power of the British empire. We do not ourselves wish to be understood, as stating positively that a war with the United States is become inevitable; the door for amicable adjustment still remains open, and while it continues so, hopes of adjustment may not irrationally be indulged. But in whatever manner the negotiation may terminate, we shall have the consolation to re-

(See 4th Page.)

Facsimile of the first extant issue of the *Missouri Gazette*

By late 1813, he had run out of paper and again had to resort to expedients. On December 11, however, he even ran out of expedients and announced that "the Editor will be compelled to suspend the publication of the Gazette for a few weeks . . . Every Saturday, a Handbill will be printed and sent to our subscribers (gratis) giving a summary of the news received by the mails." He had forwarded money for paper eastward in plenty of time "but in consequence of no regular trade being carried on with that place, his paper waits for an accidental trader coming this way." [7] The paper finally resumed publication in its full size on February 26, 1814.

Charless also had during this period the continuing problem of debtors who refused to pay. This, it may be recalled had also been one of his major difficulties both in Lewistown and in Lexington. His first reminder to subscribers that it cost money to publish the *Missouri Gazette* was made on August 20, 1809, when he invited payment for subscriptions, announcing that the editor was "much pressed for Cash and is obliged to be importunate." He repeated this invitation on January 25 of the following year. On April 19, 1810, he wrote:

The editor begs leave to inform those subscribers to the Gazette who are in arrears *almost two years*, that he is made of flesh and blood, that cameleon like he does not live on air, but endeavors to subsist like other folks . . . Postmasters . . . will not refuse receipts to those who wish to remit a few Spanish pictures to the printer.

But politeness, he found, does not always in a matter of this kind elicit response, and on July 20, the first issue of the third year of the *Gazette*'s existence, he announced that "To those who have only lent us their names, we have to request them to give us a better evidence of their wish to support the first press that has yet ascended the Mississippi." On December 19 he again pleaded for payment and pointed out that the weekly expense of publishing the *Gazette* was upwards of twenty dollars. On September 12, 1811, and again on August 8, 1812, he announced that payment of overdue accounts would be sought through legal action. By that time he had over $1,000 due him from subscribers and advertisers who were in arrears in their payments,[8] and on December 5, 1812, he animadverted through thirteen column inches of editorial on the necessity of newspaper subscribers paying their debts. Without doubt one of the most readable paragraphs ever written by an editor on the subject of his need to be paid was published by Charless in 1816. It read:

Could a printer strike sustenance from his head, as Vulcan struck Pallas from the head of Jove, then, indeed, it would be folly in him to complain; but such miracles are not to be worked now-a-days. Or could his look convert stones into flesh, as the head of Medusa did flesh into stone, he might do tolerably well. But printers unfortunately for themselves, are no magicians, altho' they deal in an *art* which has charmed mankind. They have much headwork to perform; but their teeth require to be occupied also. Indeed, with some, the occupation with the teeth is the major object. And, to confess the truth, it forms a part of our ambition also, otherwise we should not now be writing this paragraph..

In plain terms, we think ourselves full as competent to sign a receipt as write a paragraph. And we would thank those who wish us to perform the latter, to first call and take with them a specimen of the former—for like what the federalists used to say of Bonaparte, we "want money and must have it." [9]

Charless obviously never found an adequate solution to this perennial and chronic problem.

Charless was willing to accept almost any merchandisable commodity in payment for his paper. It will be recalled that he had advertised in his prospectus that the *Gazette* would be sold not only for three dollars per year in cash but also for four dollars per year in country produce, and from time to time he reminded his readers of this option that was available to them. He frequently announced his willingness to accept grain, vegetables, flour, poultry, beef, or pork, as well as gentian, sarsaparilla, and snake root.[10] It is clear from other references in the *Gazette* during this period that Charless was trafficking in many kinds of commerce that were far removed from his major profession of printing and bookselling. He sold coffee, and bacon, and cows, and he purchased barley, hops, brass, copper, cord wood, and split rails, as well as rags. On at least one occasion he peddled his services as an auctioneer.[11]

In addition to the problems that he experienced with the mails and with his subscribers, Charless had also to contend with an unstable labor force. By July 19, 1809, he had disposed of his Louisville press and had moved his entire operation from Kentucky. All his sons were apprenticed to the trade, but they were too few and too young to keep his new printing office in full operation. As was mentioned earlier, he advertised for an apprentice once in French and many other times in English. He also sought journeymen through his columns. Again Charless found the War of 1812 an especially trying period, not only because it was difficult to get news, ink, and paper from the east, but also because it reduced the number of his employees.

The principal hands imployed [sic] in our office, having marched to the defence of our frontier [Charless announced on September 5, 1812] we shall be unable to perform any other work than the Gazette: should the danger increase, the editor will also join his fellow citizens in arms; in that case, his children will issue a half sheet weekly.

Charless' sons at that time ranged from eight to seventeen years of age. Fortunately, the war did not come closer, and Charless was able to stay at his press.

By November of 1809 the paper had grown to a four-column folio sheet with pages 11 x 18 inches in size, and Charless changed its name to the *Louisiana Gazette*, but in mid-1812 he changed the name back again to make it consistent with the new official name of the territory. Despite changes in its name and other vicissitudes, however, the paper prospered during its first six years. Beginning with a small list of 174 subscribers in 1808, it could boast in 1815 of having "upwards of 500 genuine patrons, who receive it regularly every week." [12] Charless had sought diligently to extend its circulation as much as possible. In 1809 he had subscription agents employed in seven communities in the Missouri, Illinois, and Indiana territories. By 1814 the number of such agencies had been increased to fourteen, which included St. Charles, Bonhomme, Herculaneum, Potosi, Ste. Genevieve, Cape Girardeau, Byrdtown, Rosseville, Goshen, Madison, Cahokia, Walnut Grove, Kaskaskia, and Shawneetown. Late in 1809 Charless had advertised his interest in contracting with an individual to deliver his *Gazette* twice monthly to some sixty subscribers along a route "from Mr. Campbell's 'ferry, to Six Mile Prairie, through the settlements of Wood River, and Goshen to Clinton Hill." [13] Delivery of newspapers was difficult before the days of free rural mail service.

Despite these many difficulties there can be little doubt that the *Missouri Gazette* was a successful financial venture. Advertising as well as circulation increased rapidly. Whereas in the first extant issue of the *Gazette* there had been only two paid advertisements, there were in Charless' last issue on September 13, 1820, fully seventy. Birkhead has summarized the proprietor's income in 1814 as follows:

In the June, 1814, issue, which may be considered as typical of the period, there were eighty-seven inches of advertising. Most, if not all, had been inserted previously so the quoted rate would be fifty cents per inch, a total of about forty dollars worth at the rates quoted. In addition to this, the front page was entirely legal proceedings and laws passed by Congress for which Charless was also paid. It would be reasonably safe to assert that he was paid at least fifty dollars per week at the rates stated in this period.[14]

This was above, of course, his obvious income of some $2000 per annum from subscribers.

The most controversial political topic in which Charless became embroiled during his first six years in St. Louis was the disposal of old Spanish land grants under the new American government. Land had been freely distributed to settlers under the Spanish rule of the Louisiana district, and upon the surveying of these granted tracts, certificates of the survey had been issued to the grantees. For the practical purpose of holding land and transferring it by sale under the Spanish, these certificates were considered adequate, but technically they were not clear titles unless the settlers had pursued the final and complicated step of getting their concessions sanctioned by the governor general at New Orleans. Complete titles had therefore been considered quite unnecessary, and very few settlers had troubled themselves to procure them. Indeed the board of land commissioners appointed in 1832 to settle these land claims found only eighteen completed Spanish land titles in all of what had been Upper Louisiana. Immediately upon the purchase of the Louisiana Territory by the United States there was wild and extensive speculation in Spanish land claims by American opportunists, and many deeds were fraudulently altered or illegally issued involving huge land holdings.

Late in 1805 President Jefferson appointed a board of land commissioners comprised of Clement B. Penrose, John B. C. Lucas, and Frederick Bates to investigate land claims in Upper Louisiana and to pass on or deny their confirmation under the new government. This group at first felt that its instructions were to confirm all deeds that bore the slightest appearance of being legitimate resident claims, and it began its duties with this liberal viewpoint as its guide. For obvious reasons this was a popular view with both the older French residents and the early speculators. But it was equally unpopular with new residents who found unconfirmed land cheaper to purchase; this latter faction found support in the person of the United States land agent at St. Louis, William C. Carr. The land commissioners later reversed themselves and adopted Carr's rigid position. Political activity as regards land claims became very hot as influential claimants and counterclaimants petitioned the Congress for legal support of their views, and Congress responded with new laws bearing on the matter in 1805, 1806, 1807, 1812, 1813, 1814, and in subsequent years. Indeed laws continued to be enacted on these claims until 1867.[15] It is not surprising that Charless' newpaper raised its voice in such an all-embracing controversy.

As Printer to the Territory Charless was always subject to suspicion in political matters as being aligned with the party that had appointed him, but he stoutly maintained his independence. Before his *Gazette* was six months old, he had found it necessary to print denials of such accusations.

I must take this opportunity to contradict a report industriously circulated that "the gazette is under certain controul." I hereby declare the assertion to be false; should the rights or liberties of the people be invaded, the gazette, like a faithful sentinel, will ever be ready to sound an alarm: such a report at this period of repose, unanimity and confidence, must flow from a very foul source; that the propagator may before the return of another season, be found reformed tranquil and happy, is the sincere wish of

Joseph Charless[16]

Some of the unsigned communications that appeared in Charless' early columns revolved around the difficult problem of land claims. At first Charless tried to pursue a middle course, but his position on the matter was soon interpreted as being in support of the more rigid view. A series of anonymous charges and countercharges that appeared in his "Communicated" column in late 1809 signed on the one hand by "A Land Claimant" and by "Corrector" on the other, became so warm that a duel threatened, and the editor had to announce on November 30 that "The pieces of 'The Land Claimant,' and 'Corrector,' having become personal, we charge them as advertisements." In his handling of this controversy Charless made enemies with many of the wealthy old families and influential entrepreneurs who held large grants, either legitimate or fraudulent, from the pre-American period. Charless referred to this group in his editorials as the "Little Junto," and found himself siding more and more frequently with the "anti-junto," which was comprised largely of recent American settlers and new enterprisers, of whom the chief spokesmen were Rufus Easton, John B. C. Lucas, his attorney son Charles Lucas, and the popular David Barton. The differences between these two groups continued in evidence on every political question that faced the Missouri Territory from that time to statehood in 1820 and caused Charless some grievous editorial battles.

Chapter VI

A DAGGER AND SWORD CANE

On his masthead Charless carried a motto of which any Irish editor would have been proud.[1] It was "Truth without Fear." In attempting to present the truth as he saw it, he annoyed many people. Editorially he struck out with vehemence at any and all action that he felt was against the public good, disregarding party, person, or position. In his press, he assumed the role of the public conscience and pursued it impervious to implied threats of bodily harm and less-veiled efforts at economic harassment of his operation. During the first six years of his work in St. Louis many pressures, mostly subtle, were unsuccessfully brought to bear upon him to get him to adopt a more moderate tone and more tractable attitude toward what he felt were the indiscretions, the inexcusable actions or inactions, and the corruptions of the great as well as the small.

But that was the first six years. Charless' last six years as editor, from 1814 to 1820, were different. Pressures were no longer subtle, threats were no longer implied, and attacks upon him became overt rather than concealed as they had been before. The frontier was peopled by men of action, men who were accustomed to overcoming any barriers that stood in their way, whether they were wild animals, mountain ranges, bands of savage Indians, or newspaper editors. If Charless attacked them editorially, they would fight back with whatever weapons came to hand.

The War of 1812 was a particularly difficult time for Charless. In the upper Mississippi Valley it was, for the most part, a war between Indians and white settlers, and Charless was always bitter concerning Indian depredations. At best the war was a confused guerrilla conflict much of which could not be conducted by the historically received tactics of military science. Communications in the Western Country were poor, and it frequently appeared that the United States was losing the war. Indian nations were often dubious allies and, by white men's standards, unpredictable. Furthermore, the enemy was the British, than whom in the eyes of an Irish editor there could have been none more despicable. Thus Charless became emotionally involved in a series of events and circumstances that were on occasion impossible for even the clearest-headed individual properly to assess. As proprietor of one of the major information centers west of Pittsburgh, he frequently came upon intelligences not normally available to his neighbors concerning the military activities of the enemy. This information he carefully omitted from his newspaper and forwarded promptly to the Secretary of War, James Monroe. The judicious restraint that he showed in this self-censorship of his columns is explained in the last paragraphs of a letter which he wrote to Monroe in 1813:

At the time Gov. Howard left this place for Kentucky, our frontiers wore the face of tranquility, all the hostile bands had gone to Detroit or to Chicago, to the latter place they were invited by *Lagoterie* an English trader, bearing a

Wampum, he informed them that a vessel with some Cannon and white warriors, a Vast quantity of ammunition and clothing would arrive. In consequence of this assurance the Western shores of lake Michigan were covered with indians, some say 3000, I would rather suppose 12 to 1500, consisting of Winabagoes, Wild Oats, Ottawa, Chippewa, some Soux, 80 Warriors of the Sac's, a few Foxes and Aoways and almost all the Pottowatomies, Kickapoos, Miamies, Delawars, Shawonees, Piankyshaws &c. &c. of the Rock, Fox, Illinois and the other rivers which head near the lake, together with those from Old Woman and the upper branches of the Wabash Rivers. Last week we received positive information (from friendly indians) that the long expected vessel had arrived at Greenbay, 50 or 60 miles N. W. of Chicago, in company with a number of Barges bearing the promised supply. The military force comprising this expedition are said to be Barge men picked up at the upper posts, amounting to 400. Blondeau the Fox interpreter, who was at the seat of Government last summer, has just arrived here from Fort Belle vue, he reports that he saw the British Wampum at the upper indian villages, inviting them all to repair to Green bay, where they would be supplyed with every necessary and "enjoy the pleasure of seeing the Americans driven from the Mississippi by that strong arm which crushed them on the borders of the lakes."

Prudential motives have induced me to withhold giving publicity in my paper to indian movements, as the country is threatened with desertion, a great number of families are preparing to remove into Kentucky and Tennessee as soon as the weather will permit, These consist generally of the most respectable of our population. Those who remain, if they were in sufficient numbers would form a pretty strong barrier against savage inroads; They are usually termed "The Pioneers of the West," a people accustomed to a Frontier, and to Indian Warfare. The Americans of this place are confident that Government will send them immediate assistance,

They do not claim an exemption from fighting. They wish to face the enemy with a competent force, a force which cannot now be collected in the Territory.[2]

Much of the military leadership on the frontier was provided by citizen soldiers rather than by professionals, and Charless frequently felt that this leadership was mediocre in quality. He often castigated in his columns military figures who were sometimes heroes in the eyes of others. "Treason, if the following is true!" the editor had headed his article concerning the surrender of General Hull's camp at Detroit in 1812.[3] "General Howard," stated an anonymous article signed *Q in the Corner,* "as a private citizen, is worthy of esteem, but as a general, he has no pretension to our admiration." [4] Other military men were scourged with equal vigor. These men were not without their defenders, however. The article by "Q" fomented considerable excitement among the admirers of General Howard,[5] many of whom were among the "little junto" mentioned above. They insisted that "Old Charley," as the editor was sometimes called by his detractors, was again writing his own anonymous communications, and then they called him a liar when he denied it. Major William Christy, earlier the commander-in-chief of the Louisiana Territory, the above-mentioned land agent William C. Carr, quondam circuit judge who was impeached in 1832, with Clement B. Penrose, then justice of the peace, all armed, waited upon Charless one Sunday morning and demanded the identity of "Q," but the editor refused them satisfaction. Charless relates:

Before these men came to the office, they thought proper to denounce me as the author of "Q" in the last weeks Gazette, said I was a liar, &c. This kind of language was certainly not calculated to smooth the way to an amicable ecclaireissement [sic]. No, the object was to *controul* or *destroy* the *liberty* of the *Press* in this place, or why should two judges of the court of common pleas armed with a sword and a club, on a Sunday to enter rudely the Printing Office, and demand in a dictatorial manner the author of "Q" in the last paper: This style could only meet with the answer given; "I have been informed you have denounced me as the author, therefore you shall have no satisfaction from me."

My patrons may rest assured, that I shall preserve the Liberty of the Press as long as I am able to controul one, and when I become the humble tool of factious men, I shall no longer hope to merit support.

Joseph Charless [6]

But he allowed his opposition to present its case in the same issue. Obviously here was a man difficult to deal with.

It was not only military men whom Charless attacked. He also had a dire distrust of lawyers, although he sent his son Joseph to read law at Transylvania University—probably to enable him better to defend himself in later life. Lawyers, in Charless' eyes, had an unfair advantage over the populace and needed to be watched closely. Lawyers could steal, swindle, cheat, and then with an eloquent appeal to a jury and reference to statutes and cases that may or may not have existed, be turned free to do so again. Charless felt he knew this well; he was himself justice of the peace from 1812 to at least 1824. No doubt his distrust of the law dated from his early days in Ireland where he observed printers and malcontents diligently prosecuted by the Crown and convicted by biased courts for their revolutionary thinking.

Although Charless appears to have made every effort to abide by the law, his attitude toward the legal profession meant that the bar and the bench were among his enemies. They, in turn, proved that his distrust was justified by bringing suit against him on any pretext they could devise and convicting him whenever they could. It is useful to observe that two of the three men mentioned above who made the armed sortie into Charless' office were judges. Although they failed then to learn the identity of "Q," five months later they found a kind of satisfaction in the complexities of the law.

The case grew out of an Indian massacre wherein a man named Eastwood was scalped by three Osage Indians. The three Osages were imprisoned in St. Louis to await trial, and Charless, who was bitter as usual about Indian depredations, referred to the case in his columns. "We shall have the same * * * * acted here as was performed sometime ago with the Iaways and Sack Indians," the similar case mentioned above in which Charless had sat as a juryman and in which the Indians had been convicted. President Jefferson had later interested himself in that case, and on an appeal the Indians had been released.[7] "A band of savages," Charless continued, "meet a white man in the woods or plains, he is shot and his body treated with every indignity—The murderers boast of the exploit and in a style of frolick deliver themselves up for trial—They plead *not guilty* and *are acquitted.*" For printing these comments, Charless was hailed into court on a contempt charge, pleaded not guilty, but was convicted and fined $5.00. His prediction, however, proved correct; the Indians were acquitted.[8]

In the year 1814, the several parties opposed to Charless' vigorous editorializing began to consider fight-

ing fire with fire. Why should they not establish an
opposition press—one which would present their side of
an argument? On April 16 of that year they entered an
advertisement in the Lexington *Reporter.* "To Printers,"
it read, "The people of *St. Louis* are desirous of procuring
a printer at that place. A man of correct republican principles, with even moderate abilities would satisfy them."
Charless reprinted the announcement in his own paper
with the observation that "It is a well known fact, that
the *people of St. Louis,* audaciously styled as above, consist of only *five* or *six* individuals: and that the Editor of
the Missouri Gazette does meet with the decided approbation of the PEOPLE of ST. LOUIS, the *little*
lawyer, and *would be* Lord Mayor, to the contrary notwithstanding." [9]

Since Charless' *Gazette* was exchanged for most of the
other papers in the nation, there can be little doubt that
his comments upon the opportunity for another printer
in St. Louis did much to discourage one from going there.
But the efforts of the opposition continued. Seven months
later Charless referred again to its hopes of establishing
a new press as follows:

A committee has been appointed to procure a loan from the
military and such citizens who can be prevailed upon to
part with their money, on loan, to the new Printer, and *one*
of the *editors* of the *Kaskaskia newspaper* is employed to
print for them.

The party in this place, declare at the head of their subscription list, that they wish to procure a printer of "moderate
republican principles," that is, in plain language, a printer
who will shut his eyes to every blot in the career of the junto,
and be alive to the least aberration of others in this community.[10]

By early 1815 there was another printer on the ground. A loan of $1000 was raised from among Charless' adversaries, and a young attorney named Joshua Norvell who had been a junior editor on the *Illinois Herald* of Kaskaskia was brought in to establish a new press. Charless invited the new paper to publish a list of its subscribers in an early issue. "It will be well," he told his readers, "to notice who are *judges*, lawyers, officers of the United States army, or militia among them." [11]

Charles observed the arrival of Norvell in St. Louis and the efforts of the men who had brought him there in an entertaining letter to Ninian Edward, Governor of the Illinois Territory. It read in part as follows:

We have very little news here at this time, except that the arrival of a new printer, brought on by Christy, Carr & Farrar, can be noticed. *Maj.* Christy told Dr. Simpson *they wanted a good printer,* &c., &c. Now to give you a specimen of the literary acquirements of this learned critic, I will beg leave to refer you to the subjoined letter of the Major—in his best style.

Very respectfully,
Jos. Charless.[12]

Verbatem ad literatem

(Amusement)   Sunday—17th April, '14

Sir

Yur sons and apprentice Boys are almost dayley in the habit of runing through my field treading my young wheet and Clover, & Shooting fowls in my Pond I have more then once forbid them doing so but in vain—If you do not think propir to put a stop to these depradations I shall be under the nicessity of taking such steps as will

Yr & C
W Christy

Mr J. Charless

ERRATA

For yur	read your	For propir	read proper
" dayley	read daily	" depradation	read depredation
" runing	read running	" nicessity	read necessity
" then	read than		
" forbid	read forbade		
" wheet	read wheat		

The threat of competition from a second newspaper in St. Louis was probably good for Charless. He ordered out a new, larger press and some new fonts of type. He made vigorous efforts to extend his subscription list, but he also continued to chastise the military whenever he felt it was justified. In April 1815 he attacked what appeared to be military indecision in a punitive raid following a massacre at Cote sans Dessein. His report on Major Taylor Berry's peace mission to the Sacs was such that Berry later felt is was necessary to publish a pamphlet in his own defense.

By June Norvell's opposition newspaper was publishing under the style of the *Western Journal*. The *Gazette*, in anonymous columns signed "St. Louis School Boy," bitterly attacked Norvell, and Norvell counterattacked in kind. William C. Carr especially used the new paper for letters to the editor in which he castigated Charless, and Charless fought back at him also. Finally on July 21, 1815, Charless reprinted in a broadside the sequence of rejoinders and surrejoinders that had taken place between himself and Carr. A day later Charless reported the following:

Yesterday evening, when I was conversing with some gentlemen near the post-office of St. Louis, William C. Carr approached close to me, without my observing him, and spit in my face, and at the same instant drew a pistol and presented it towards me. Being altogether unarmed, not even a stick in my hand, I had no other resort but stoneing him, from which I was soon prevented by individuals, who interfered and laid hold of me, which gave Carr an opportunity of retreating to his house, no doubt exulting at his own *brave* and manly management of the affair, and at the strong proof he had given of his being a *gentleman* and a soldier.

During 1816 the asperity between the junto and the antijunto increased. Both sides were strong, but if the number of subscribers can be used as a gauge, the support of the populace in St. Louis was enjoyed by Charless and his faction. The *Gazette* continued to grow in size and circulation, whereas the *Western Journal* experienced much difficulty, going through three changes of title and nine editors during the first decade of its existence. A particularly acrimonious debate took place in the two papers during this year concerning the candidacy as territorial delegate to the Congress of John Scott of Ste. Genevieve. Again the *Gazette* printed anonymous columns concerning Scott at which he took violent offense, demanding the identity of their author. Charless gave Scott five names, and Scott challenged them all to duels, but they all refused. After a bitter campaign, winner Scott was refused a congressional seat pending the outcome of fraud proceedings against him, and a new election was ordered. Scott won this election as well, but during his subsequent four-year stay in Washington, he stubbornly refused to send to Charless any reports on congressional activities, although Charless pointed out on several occasions that readers of his *Gazette* were equally as important to Scott's continuing support as

delegate as were readers of the opposition newspaper.
Apparently Scott was never able to see the truth of this
assertion, for the *Missouri Gazette* thereafter had to rely
on other sources of information concerning events in the
national capital.

The military had ways of getting its licks in against
Charless in return for his jibes at them. Even the recruiting sergeant got into the game, for on the night of August
4, 1817, he "in company with the musick of a recruiting
party came to my house, about midnight," [the editor
wrote] "after the election followed by a mob of incon-
siderate young men, playing the 'rogue's march,' and
whooping and hallooing the indian yell; throwing stones
at my house." [13] The commanding officer of the recruiting
party faced a court martial for allowing his band to par-
ticipate in this mob scene, but Charless' suspicion both
of the military and of legal justice was again fortified
when he was acquitted. He would have been heartened
to know that, despite the acquittal, President Monroe
himself wrote to General Thomas A. Smith, commanding
the troops in Missouri, expressing his concern over the
military having been so much in evidence on that election
day, but Charless probably never knew of the letter.[14]

Four weeks later a young man named Carter Copeland
came to Charless' house and requested the identity of
the author of still another anonymous letter in the *Gazette*, this one concerning the impending elections in
Kentucky. Charless again refused to tell.

Next day [wrote Charless] after breakfast, the young man
appeared in the Office, with a dagger and sword cane, and
demanded in a dictatorial manner the author of the letter—
he was again informed he could not be gratified,—and after a
pause of several minutes, he very modestly declared that,

'as I was roughly handled here, he did not wish to have any difficulties with me!—and immediately on the back of this declaration, he said that the author and publisher of the letter, were d————d villians, &c.' He was then ordered to walk out of the Office, and on his refusal, I accompanied him half way to the door, when he wheeled round and drew a dagger and sword cane, and made a pass at me & declared he 'would be the instant death of me.' In the interim, the young gentlemen, then in the office, got him out, and on my looking out at the door to see if he was gone, he threw a stone at my head, which I with difficulty evaded, and then, and not until then, (although reported otherwise) I fired at him. The pistol was some time charged—it hung fire—and I am happy to say, the life of an intemperate youth has been saved.[15]

The next person to wield a weapon against editor Charless will forever remain anonymous. On August 28, 1818, the printer recorded in his *Gazette* that "On Tuesday night last, about nine o'clock, the editor of this paper while walking in his garden was fired at by some villain who had concealed himself in or behind the south lot of the garden. The bullet struck within a few steps of its intended victim and in the range of the walk he had a few minutes before left." Being an editor in those days had its physical dangers.

Chapter VII

STATEHOOD AND ABOLITION

In 1815 Charless saw a great man arrive in St. Louis from Tennessee: a man of dominant will and commanding disposition. The man was both a military officer and an attorney, so editor Charless was not surprised to see him throw his great bulk to the cause of the enemy. This new arrival was Colonel Thomas Hart Benton, hero of the War of 1812, who had become unwelcome in Nashville after he and his brother had wounded General Andrew Jackson in a feud. Soon after his arrival in St. Louis Colonel Benton lost a court case to a popular young lawyer named Charles Lucas, son of John B. C. Lucas. After exchanging insults a challenge was sent, the two met at dawn on a sandbar in the Mississippi River called Bloody Island because it was a favorite dueling spot, and Lucas was killed. Charless, who was both a close friend of Lucas and a violent opponent of dueling, was further embittered toward Benton by this event. He later described the event as he saw it in a letter to the antislavery leader John W. Taylor. Benton, he explained, had been

... selected by the "Violents" to bring out young Lucas and send him to out of this troublesome world. The public here appreciate him as he ought to be—It is well known that he

105

called Lucas to the fatal spot armed with potent breech'd pistols, instruments so curiously made as to throw a ball into the victim, before poor Lucas' ball could reach him. The quarrel was originally between John Scott & Lucas, but he had not nerve to meet the deadly combat—it was left for Benton . . . to terminate that business—it is also known that young Lucas offered every apology to B. and was to submit the affair to a court of *honor* and abide its decisions. Mr. B. wishes to fill a senators chair and will go through thick & thin to obtain it.[1]

Charless was even further annoyed the following year when Benton and several other dissatisfied stockholders in the Bank of St. Louis walked into the bank and physically took charge of it and ran it for a time while an ineffectual constabulary stood by and watched helplessly. Charless, who was also a stockholder in the bank but who sided with the satisfied majority, was understandably chagrined at these actions on the part of the Tennessee colonel.

Benton's opinion of "Old Charley" was at least as bad as Charless' was of Benton. By 1819 Charless' old mentor and creditor Mathew Carey had turned the muddled financial affairs of his publishing house over to his more methodical son for operation. The son, Henry C. Carey, took on, as one of his early tasks, the collection of all old debts that appeared to be due the firm. Among them he found an apparent indebtedness by Charless, and he retained Thomas Hart Benton as his solicitor to handle its collection. Benton presented the demand to Charless in St. Louis who of course denied that he owed the Philadelphians a penny. "This answer however is with me no evidence of the injustice of your demand," reported Benton to the Careys,[2] "as Mr. Charless will answer any

claim in the same way, and pay nothing . . . until pressed
into it. I will therefore sue him for you if you have proof
of your account." It is not known if the Philadelphia
house was unable to muster adequate evidence of their
account or if the editor settled without benefit of legal
action, but there is no record that the alacrity with which
Benton volunteered to sue Charless ever got the Irishman
into court. It was no doubt a great disappointment to the
Tennessean.

From Charless' viewpoint the worst conceivable event
took place in August of 1818. Thomas Hart Benton,
soldier, attorney, murderer of Charless' good friend, and
supporter of the junto, became editor of the opposition
newspaper and changed its name to the St. Louis
Enquirer. From that time until 1820 when Missouri became a state and Benton was elected to the U.S. Senate
where he served for a quarter-century, Charless and
Benton carried on a vitriolic although not unentertaining
war of wits and words.

For two years the editors agreed on only one thing:
mail service was poor. On every other subject they dis-
agreed almost automatically. They blamed one another
for all ills, they harassed one another, they twitted and
taunted and scolded. Benton finally wrote Charless a
letter prohibiting him from ever printing Benton's name
in the *Gazette* again, "except for purposes of scandal and
defamation." Charless printed the letter. Thereafter he
only alluded to the colonel indirectly or punned on his
name: "The Enquirer-man," he wrote, "*bent-on* mischief."
In August of 1819 Benton accused Charless editorially of
having made up fully one hundred lies about John Scott,
the *Enquirer*'s candidate for the Senate. The *Gazette* insisted that Benton itemize them. Benton promptly pro-

duced a column entitled "List of One Hundred Lies Fabricated by the Old Communications Maker," numbering quotations 1, 2, 3, 4, 5, and so forth right on up to one hundred. By late 1819 relations between the two men had come to a total stand. Benton wrote a brief note to Charless. "Mr. Joseph Charless," it read, "will discontinue my subscription to his newspaper. Thomas H. Benton, October 30, 1819." Again Charless printed the letter.

Despite the effect that the editorial dueling had on the participants, it was undeniably good for business. By 1819 the *Gazette* could boast a subscription list containing one thousand names, just double what it had been four years earlier. The paper had now six columns to the page and employed agents in twenty-seven communities in the Missouri Territory and eight in Illinois. The junto and antijunto continued, however, to torment one another. On January 1, 1819, an unsigned advertisement was run in Charless' *Gazette* which read as follows. "D. Kimball requests the incendiaries of St. Louis to defer burning Mr. Charless' establishment, until his removal, which will be on the 20th April next." But Charless was not removing. In October he recorded:

The history of our establishment for the last 11 years would present an interesting and singular detail. It would exhibit violence, persecution, arrogance and unprincipled ambition; in many instances connected with power, all arrayed against us. We have been attacked repeatedly, abused and slandered, both by men in power and men out of power . . .

Our course in the Gazette has been an impartial one, without fear of any one. A bold and impudent visage and a pompous strut has never frightened us, nor the fear of the dirk or of the duelling pistol alarmed us. The God of Nature and the woods of Missouri furnished us with sufficient defence against

the attacks of all open assailants or midnight assassins. The
same impartial and fearless course we have ever pursued we
shall continue to pursue, as long as we conduct the paper.
When we discover that plagiarism, impudence, arrogance,
and partiality are preferred by the people of Missouri, to
plain, honest, unvarnished truth, we shall sell out and quit.
Till then we shall hold on.[3]

The next twelve months, however, were rough ones
for Charless, because important problems were arising for
the Missouri Territory. The advantages and disadvan-
tages of statehood were being debated, but more controversial than statehood itself was the slavery issue. If
Missouri were to be admitted to the Union as a state,
should it be slave or free? Newspapers the country over
were editorializing upon the fate of Missouri, and the two
most caustic in expressing their views of the problem
were the St. Louis *Enquirer,* which was for continued
slavery, and the *Missouri Gazette,* which was for abolition. Some of the bitterest fulminations in the history of
journalism dripped from their columns. Several strongly
antislave articles were published in the *Missouri Gazette*
in 1819, signed "A Farmer of St. Charles County." They
were highly literate and coherent arguments against
human bondage, quoting the great philosophers. Other
articles followed, proposing different solutions: total and
immediate emancipation, gradual emancipation, emancipation of female slaves, and discontinuation of slave im-
ports; all that appeared in the *Gazette* were antislave
in basic philosophy. The *Enquirer,* meanwhile, assumed
a proslavery stance and was supported as usual by the
people who had formerly comprised the junto.

Several public meetings were called during the year
ostensibly to air the problem of Missouri's proposed ad-

mission to the Union, but the bondage issue was always in the forefront of the discussion. On April 11, 1820, Charless himself acted as chairman of a St. Louis meeting where resolutions were adopted asking for the discontinuance of Negro importation or immigration into Missouri.[4] Charless reported that it was a public meeting with some one hundred people in attendance, but his account was called into question by a report published four days later by the *Enquirer*. Four young men, it stated, who were known to be supporters of the slavery cause, had tried to attend the meeting, which was held at Maury's old hotel, and watch the debate, but Joseph Charless had met them at the door and had informed them that

"No person who was not in favor of restricting slavery," or words to that effect, "ought to be in that meeting, and that no others were invited." Upon one of those who were present, remarking in reply, that this was understood to be a public meeting and that he would not leave the room except upon the principle that the Meeting was private, Mr. Joseph Charless informed him that "he had hired the room for the night and bought the candles."[5]

upon which the young men left. They claimed that there were only some forty people present rather than one hundred.

When the election was finally held in May, 1820, however, it was clear that Charless and his abolitionist colleagues had suffered a severe defeat. St. Louis County polled only 2,026 votes for restricting slavery as opposed to 7,265 votes for the proslavery faction.[6] The editor took his defeat gracefully.

We are contented [he wrote] We never wish to interfere

with the will of the people clearly and distinctly expressed. Although we shall at times conceive it our duty to leave our columns open for the free discussion of all subjects, still we feel little disposition to a further examination of the subjects which we conceive now settled by the people.[7]

Although Charless discontinued at that time editorializing upon slavery itself, he continued lambasting Benton and his two co-proprietors of the *Enquirer*, the young Isaac N. Henry, and an older man named Evarist Maury. It even appears that Charless at this time abandoned the principles he had outlined in the original prospectus to the *Gazette* and did indeed "follow a man into the circle of private life," printing what was no doubt the most direct personal attack of his career in journalism. The attack was occasioned by criticisms that appeared in the *Enquirer* of certain gospel ministers who had lent their talents to the cause of abolition during the campaign. Charless countered by asking, also in the issue of May 10: "Is the right to engage in the discussion of the question of slavery and give an opinion upon it, really confined and secured to none but an *old, sinful, obdurate batchelor, a father of negroes, and a murderer?*"

The closing phrases, italicized by Charless, may be interpreted as referring to Maury, Henry, and Benton respectively, and must have been calculated to elicit a violent response from them. If that was their purpose, they were successful, for two hours after their publication the two editors came to blows.

The Editor of the Missouri Gazette [quoting from the subsequent issue of the *Gazette*] whilst on the way from his office to his house, between one and two o'clock, on Wednesday the 10th of May inst. was assailed, as he ascended the hill, without any previous intimation, warning, or apparent quarrel, by Isaac N. Henry, one of the Editors of the St. Louis Enquirer, and receiving several blows with a heavy cudgell, which blows he returned with a stick disproportionately small; the cambatants closed, fell, and struggled for a while. The Rev. Joseph Piggott, who was accompanying Mr. Charless, and was going to dine with him, twice endeavored to part them, but was as often prevented by a certain Wharton Rector, who drew a pistol from his bosom, and declared he would blow him through, if he interfered. Mr. Piggott then called for help, being determined to part them; presently two men came up and the contest ended.

In the same issue Charless repeated his insult of Henry, by publishing an anonymous column signed "An Admirer of Modern Times." This column recommended that Henry and other young bachelors get married, asking "Have they not their house keepers, and their little ones also?"

Henry's attack on Charless gained national notoriety and was reported in newspapers in other parts of the country. Everywhere Henry's attack was interpreted as having been inspired by the slavery issue rather than by Charless' insult. Northern newspapers especially, such as the *Berks and Schuylkill Journal* of Reading, Pennsylvania, rewrote the article from the *Gazette* and gave it wider circulation. The New York *Daily Advertiser*,[8] after pointing out that Charless was attacked by two young men whose aggregate ages did not total the Irishman's fifty years, went on to report that "Mr. C. used the shilelah to great advantage, and when the battle ended, the amount of damage sustained fell upon Mr. Henry, whose shoulder was unjointed." The *Enquirer* was highly annoyed at the wide publicity which the incident received and on July 26 editorialized upon it.

Thus the personal dispute between two individuals in this town was first swelled into a design to murder an old man because he was opposed to slavery, and now the character of the country is blackened with the same crime. "Missourian Liberality!"—And thus an individual lie is made to attach to a population of 100,000 souls.

The truth or falsehood of Charless' slur on Henry's character is not now determinable.

Charless was seldom given to seeking satisfaction in courts of law, but he did so in the case of Henry's attack. A warrant was issued on the same day as the attack, and in August an indictment was found against Henry. On September 13, 1820, he was found guilty of assault and was fined. Charless, however, should have kept out of court, for the law, he learned to his distress, is a two-edged sword. On the same day as his assailant was fined, Colonel Thomas Hart Benton made out an affidavit that Charless' newspaper account of the attack had appeared after criminal prosecution had been begun by Charless against Henry, "and that the said publication was in some particulars false." Charless was again hailed into court on a contempt charge and was again convicted. "He was sentenced to pay a fine of twenty dollars and the costs, and to stand committed until the sentence was complied with. The record states that he was committed to the custody of the sheriff, and . . . that he remained for some time in prison, before the fine was paid." [9]

Also on the same day as Henry's conviction, Charless retired from publishing and sold the *Missouri Gazette* to one James C. Cummings, ending many hectic years as a frontier printer. Thereafter Charless made only one last feeble effort to find the law on his side. On October 16, 1820, a memorial from Charless was presented to the

First General Assembly of the Missouri House of Representatives "praying a law to be passed on the subject of contempt of court by publication." Nine days later the House Judiciary Committee, to which the memorial had been referred, reported back that "in their opinion no new act of Legislation is necessary to be had at present, on that subject," a viewpoint concurred in by the House.[10] Charless was probably not surprised. Most of those people in the legislature were lawyers or soldiers and could not be expected to enact a law restricting their right to torment a printer.

In the *Missouri Gazette* of September 13, 1820, Joseph Charless published his valedictory to the publishing industry. The document deserves reprinting here in its entirety:

TO MY PATRONS. This number closes the 12th year since the establishment of the Missouri Gazette, in St. Louis, and with it, closes my editorial labours. A few plain remarks will not be considered ill-natured or out of place, and if any should be offended at them, all that I can say is, that I have always claimed and exercised the right to think, & act for myself, and do not feel disposed to abandon the right at the moment of closing my editorial career.

This paper was established, when the country, now composing the State of Missouri, was thinly settled and indeed scarcely contained 12,000 inhabitants.—It had been ceded but a few years. The original subscription to the Gazette was 170, and the advertising patronage was very small. My means were limited, and the establishment supported with difficulty even itself, placing out of view the support of a large and growing family.—Gratitude here demands an acknowledgement, which is most sincerely made, for the assistance, friendship and patronage of some valuable supporters, some of whom still survive, but most of whom have gone to their rest, and receive the reward of their virtues in another world. There are also many other individuals to whom I feel real gratitude for their continual support, and their prompt and punctual discharge of their dues—But while I express these feelings which are due, I must also state, that the Gazette establishment has had to encounter the most violent hostility, which has sometimes even extended to my personal interests, and nothing but prudence, attention, and perseverance has preserved the office from absolute ruin.

During a considerable part of the time from the commencement of this paper, in 1808, to the present time, the most violent party spirit has raged in the town of Saint Louis.—The most violent measures have been resorted to by an overbearing aristocratic faction. Shooting, caning, and every kind of personal injury and abuse have been attempted. Sometimes young men scarcely arrived to manhood, and sometimes companies of old men, were the instruments employed by faction. —The only charge, which was made against the management of the Gazette was an independent exposure of their mercenary schemes and plots.—If it had supported their sinister and surreptitious views, it would have received their support and patronage. On this point, I do not speak from conjecture, but from facts. I have been offered by some of the principal men of this party, that I should receive their united assistance provided I would advocate their measures, & close my columns against all their opponents. An offer on my part to leave the paper open to all, was not enough. It must be exclusively theirs.—But the paper has been able to withstand their opposition and the Editor can retire, from the bustle of party strife, with moderate means for his future support, and at all events, with the satisfaction that he has acted an independent course and has never become the tool of a faction.

During several years of war and savage inroad, the paper was still continued and although surrounded by a young family and with every thing to fear—while many of our neighbours, who now roll in splendour, and live in superb buildings, left their adopted country and offered their property at any sacrifice—We did not desert our post, but kept our ground.

This establishment has lived through a period in which to be called the friend of old Charless, and to be a supporter of his paper, was considered equal to high treason, and whoever had the effrontery to presume to do either, was marked as a victim for deliberate destruction—It has lived through a period, when the private circle was invaded by the libeller and slanderer, for the purpose of retailing his half-heard tale to his credulous master. The Gazette has lived through a period, when a deliberate conspiracy could be formed to murder the man who dared to oppose a faction. It has survived the period when the person and the domestic comforts of the Editor have been most wantonly assailed—when he has been abused by Colonels, by Majors, and by Captains, by officers of government, and by private citizens.

But one consolation through these periods of difficulty and trouble still remained—all this was under a territorial government, where the officers were appointed abroad by persons, who were unable to see the exercise of the powers which they gave. It was a consolation to think that the termination of this state of things must soon arrive, and that the time would come, when the people would put down the party who ruled through the dirk & the pistol, and that the government of law and reason would ensue. That day has arrived, so long looked for and expected. Missouri has become a free and independent state and the people in assuming the government of themselves, have taught aristocrats a plain lesson of truth and have placed in the government of the state, "the man of the people."

I am now contented to retire from my labors and depart in peace. The great work is done. But I cannot suffer this opportunity to pass without touching on two subjects.

It has been said that Govs. Lewis and Howard,[11] have been

slandered in the Gazette. The charge is boldly denied, and
has been denied heretofore, and the accuser has been challenged to prove it, but he has not attempted to do so. He
therefore stands convicted of falsehood and to show his own
deformity and baseness, at the same time, he makes this
accusation, he himself slanders Gov. Howard, but cautiously
puts it in a language, which many of the friends of Gov.
Howard cannot read. But the tongue of the slanderer is equal
to the loudest hosannahs.

It has been said that the Gazette advocated the restriction
of Missouri by Congress. The base fabricator of this charge
is defied to prove it. Examine the files and they will be found
to pursue one uniform course. Open to all decent communications, the editor has never hesitated to state his opposition to
the interference of Congress, but still felt desirous that some
limitation should be put *by the People*, to the importation of
slaves.

Having thus given a sketch of the situation of this establishment, since its commencement and of the course it has pursued, nothing remains but to give some useful advice on
parting.

The Governor elect is congratulated on his almost unanimous election, which is the surest pledge of the affection and
confidence of the people. An impartial and independent
course cannot fail to insure him the gratitude of the whole
community.

Governor Clark,[12] now he is no longer the rallying point of
an overbearing faction, merits the best wishes of the community for his welfare, and ought to receive their esteem
as an amiable and virtuous citizen; and should he commence
a new political course, a reliance on his merits *alone,* should
be his only hope of acquiring confidence, & he should depre-
cate the friendship of his present supporters, and exclaim
"Heaven preserve me from my friends, as to enemies they
will do me justice."

My colleague, the co-editor of the Enquirer, is advised to

improve the hint given him about a year ago, to make a retreat to Texas. He will save time by a sudden retreat—for he
may rest assured, that the people estimate his character and
talents too truly ever to send him to the Senate of the United
States.[13] There is, it is true, one other recourse for the co-
editor—a retreat to Edwardsville, where his friend, the ex-
governor Edwards[14] may aid in completing the great road
which they have so successfully begun. After laying out the
U. S. road, through the Sangamo pre-emptions and Peoria
claims, it may be worked to Galveztown and Barrataria. The
interest of the two friends will be thus united. Co-adjustors
can be procured from the two latter places to aid in executing
the projects of these two philosophical speculators. And after
consummating all their honest plans, and the ex-governor
shall have finished his Senatorial career, they can pass hand
in hand, to the Elk-heart Grave, and spend the remainder
of their lives in dignified retirement.

Brother Type of the Enquirer,[15] cannot sustain the establishment alone. Let him, therefore, improve his hand writing, and intercede for the office of Recording Secretary to the
two friends.

The two great men of the West, Green and Findlay[16] are
advised to guard the public money, and never to pay, for
the service of the state, to any member of their faction, more
than five times as much money as the service is worth.

The little dogs of faction are advised to abandon politics,
and attend to some more certain pursuit:—at least until they
shall get a leader more competent to conduct them, than the
would-be senator.

For my fellow-citizens of Missouri, I prophecy every political happiness they can desire under the government of a man
of their choice—a man whom they know, and who will attend
to their wishes. And I know the period will soon arrive when
the greatness and the wealth of Missouri will equal that of
any state of the Union. She only needs to pay a due regard
to her own interests, and to establish correct and judicious

regulations for her own government to render her great and powerful.

Fellow Citizens and Patrons, my interests, although I leave this establishment, is still connected with yours. For 12 years I have lived among you. My family has been educated and brought up among you. My little property is in this state. Here are the tombs of my children, and here I expect to rest myself, when the cares and vexations of life are over. You must therefore believe me, when I say that nothing is, nothing can be so dear to me as your prosperity, and your welfare.

Joseph Charless

St. Louis, Sept. 13, 1820.

Chapter VIII

PRINTER TO THE TERRITORY

Charless not only relinquished the proprietorship of his newspaper in the fall of 1820 but also gave up at that time all interest in his book and job press. Actually, his book and job work had been, during his stay in Missouri, a much smaller part of his total operation than it had been in Pennsylvania and Kentucky. He maintained his official status as Printer to the Territory until 1819 and had, of course, to perform the work attendant upon that office, but his other Missouri printing was very slight. He began again issuing annual almanacs in 1817, and he printed a big book the following year in Henry S. Geyer's *Digest of the Laws of Missouri Territory,* which totaled over 550 pages. Unofficially, however, and outside these two works, he printed only a handful of broadsides and pamphlets, which included Frederick Bates's nineteen-page oration in 1809 and an exposition of the differences between Charles Lucas and John Scott in a twenty-four-page pamphlet by the former, addressed in 1816 *To the People of Missouri Territory.* He also printed in 1820 a thirty-two-page description of the *Western Land Agency and Commission Office* by Abraham Beck and an eight-page *Report of the Board of Managers of the United Society for the Spread of the Gospel.*

Except for a short time during the War of 1812 when, because of the shortage of hands, Charless had to discontinue all work other than his *Gazette*, he does not seem to have made a conscious effort to restrict his book press; indeed there is some indication that he sought to expand it. In the same season that he announced his major hands having marched to war, he was also writing to Ninian Edwards, then governor of the Illinois Territory, proposing that he be commissioned to print the laws of that territory as he was already printing those of Missouri. He informed the governor that he was prepared to print two hundred copies of the Illinois laws, one hundred pages each, for $136. Edwards was visiting in St. Louis at the time the proposal was made. Nine months later Charless repeated his offer to the governor and pointed out that he was well equipped to handle such a contract both because he had had much experience printing legal work and also because he had at that time a young printer who could be put to work on the task immediately.[1] Apparently nothing came of the proposal, however, because the Illinois laws were never printed by Charless.

It was required by statute in the early days of the Union that new laws of the United States be published in newspapers in all parts of the country as soon as possible following their passage by the Congress, and Charless long enjoyed official patronage of this kind from the federal government. As long as he had the only newspaper in the region there was no question but that the Secretary of State would regularly reimburse him for reprinting the U.S. laws. As soon, however, as Norvell established a second press in St. Louis, the faction that he represented began a five-year battle to relieve Charless of this source of income. No sooner was the ink dry on Norvell's first issues than he sent them to the Secretary of State petitioning that he be appointed public printer.[2] Despite pressure from his supporters, this did not at that time take place. Following the election of John Scott to the Congress, efforts to unseat Charless from this preferment were redoubled. Charless, on January 24, 1818, addressed the Secretary in his own defense as follows:

Sir

Two characters of this Territory, now at Washington City, had declared before they left this place, that the Missouri Gazette should no longer publish the laws of the United States—

These characters are my personal enemies, implacably intent on injuring me, because I differed in opinion with them at our last election for delegate—However, they cannot deny that I have for the last ten years, in this place, published the laws of the U. States as well as all other public acts of the government promptly—That the Gazette office—the first printing establishment in this Territory, has a circulation beyond the paper patronized by the successful party, of only seven months standing—That the Gazette has always sustained a republican character and that my opponent is of a different political character.[3]

Four days later the Secretary of State compromised the problem by appointing Sergeant Hall, who had succeeded Norvell as editor of the *Enquirer*, a second public printer in the Missouri Territory.[4] Scott was not wholly satisfied in having Hall a second public printer. He wanted Charless put out of the position and was still complaining two years later of his continuance in this patronage position.[5] Since the Secretary of State reimbursed public printers "at the rate of one dollar for each printed page . . . in the size of the sheet and type, in a manner to cor-

respond with the late revised edition of the laws, published by Bioren and Co.," [6] it may be seen that theirs
could be a profitable appointment. Despite the politicking
of his enemies, however, Charless was able to maintain
his appointment to the end.

His official position as the Missouri territorial printer
supplied Charless' press ·with a considerable amount of
work through the years. In addition to small job tasks
which he was from time to time called upon to perform, he
had also the responsibility annually of publishing the laws
enacted during the previous session of the territorial
legislature. When his was the only press in the territory,
he had no more competition for this contract than he did
for federal patronage, but following Norvell's arrival in
1815 the legislature sought bids. His first year in town
Norvell offered to print the laws for $.90 per page for
three hundred copies, whereas Charless bid $1.00.[7] Al-
though his bid was higher, Charless got the contract,
probably because Norvell's press had not yet actually
arrived in St. Louis, and it was not known that he would
actually be able to deliver the printing. The following
year Norvell bid $1.00 per page for three hundred copies,
but this time Charless hedged and proposed doing the
work for "such sum per page as the general assembly may
deem sufficient or as low as any other printer may propose
to print them for." [8] Since the same William C. Carr who
had earlier engaged Charless in fisticuffs was at that time
chairman of the House Committee on Ways and Means,
which was responsible for arranging the printing, it is
surprising to note that Charless received the contract that
year and printed the 143-page book. For his official printing during 1816 Charless received $224.42.[9]

Politics played a principal role in the summer of 1820
in the granting of the contract for the constitution and

journals of the new state's constitutional convention. On the legislative committee responsible for determining the official printer at that time was the interesting figure, Duff Green, who had somehow earned the right to wear with impunity the title of General, had been land speculator *par excellence*, and was currently the *Enquirer's* agent in Chariton, Missouri. General Green was himself destined to be editor of the *Enquirer* in 1824 and 1825 before he removed to the nation's capital to become a highly influential member of Andrew Jackson's "kitchen cabinet." Now, however, when it became the erstwhile general's responsibility to take bids on the infant state's printing, he rushed out to Isaac N. Henry's *Enquirer* office, brought in a bid of $1,100, and reported "that the committee had received proposals from the printers in St. Louis, and recommended those of I. N. Henry and Co. as the best offer." Actually this was his only offer, as the other printer in St. Louis, namely Joseph Charless, had not been invited to bid at all. Upon learning that the work was to be done, Charless submitted an uninvited proposal to do for $120 the same work Henry had offered to do for $1,100,[10] but Henry had already got the contract. When the difference in these bids was made public, the *Enquirer* could only muster, in its defense, an attack upon one specific item in Charless' bid. Wherein he had said he would do the required binding for $2.75, the *Enquirer* had sublet the binding for $36.00. "This item," obfuscated the *Enquirer*, referring to Charless' bid, "therefore contains falsehood in a proportion to truth as $36 is to $2.75, that is to say in proportion of 13 to 1." [11] It was just six weeks after this bit of boondoggling that "Old Charley" decided to retire from the printing trade and sold his office and newspaper.

Chapter IX

HOSTELER AND APOTHECARY

During his life in St. Louis, both before and after his retirement from printing, Charless made many contributions of his energy and leadership to the development of civic facilities in that place. In his newspaper columns, to be sure, he gave much free publicity to deserving civic enterprises, and, thanks in part to his efforts, St. Louis came during this period to have both a market house and a library. He also gave generously of his time. From at least as early as 1812 throughout most of the balance of his life he served as justice of the peace. In 1818 he acted as president of the Mechanics Benevolent Society, and the following year he was appointed to the standing committee of the Erin Benevolent Society. He was active in Masonic affairs, although the minutes of Missouri Lodge No. 1 indicate that he was suspended therefrom on February 3, 1824. The cause is not listed. He is credited in some quarters with having aided considerably in the establishment both of the First Methodist Church and Christ's Church Episcopal in St. Louis, and his wife Sarah is known to have been one of the founders of the First Presbyterian Church. His early efforts to become an elected public official seem to have uniformly failed— he ran for the territorial legislature in 1812 and trustee of the city in 1819—but he did serve as president of the board of aldermen of St. Louis in 1825 and 1826. All in all, Charless appears to have been what is often referred to as "a solid citizen."

During his stay in St. Louis Charless never relied upon his printing office to supply him his entire livelihood, but he rather dabbled in many other kinds of businesses and enterprises. When he had been only two years in the city he was offering ten acres of oats to Pierre Chouteau,[1] and, as was pointed out above, he trafficked in those early years in many kinds of commodities, sometimes by choice and sometimes because it was the only way he could exact payment for his services. In 1815 he announced his entry into a new business and opened an office for the registry and sale of slaves, town lots, and lands, and offered to trade bonded servants, cash bonds, or money for real property in the territory.[2] Thereafter he published advertisements with considerable frequency offering to buy and sell real estate, slaves, and other properties. He also indicated his willingness to lend money.

In 1812 Charless became involved in still another kind of business that appears today to be rather far afield from the major interests of his life, and, although his entry into that business was at that time short-lived, it was to have a great impact upon both his own future and that of St. Louis. On January 18 of that year an advertisement was published in the *Gazette* over the names of Joseph Charless and Dr. Bernard Gaines Farrar, first American physician to practice in the trans-Mississippi west, that they had opened an apothecary shop adjoining the printing office where they would have on hand a wide variety of drugs and medicine, both retail and wholesale. Two weeks later they announced their ability to supply sixty-seven vari-

eties of drugs and sixteen patent medicines. To that time
the only apothecary shops known on that part of the
frontier were the saddlebags of the traveling practitioner,
and Charless and Farrar's business must have been widely
patronized. On May 10, however, the partnership between the two men was suddenly broken [3] for reasons
not known today. For a short time thereafter Charless
continued to sell drugs at the old stand, and Dr. Farrar
opened another shop below Major Christy's tavern. By
later that year Charless appears to have discontinued his
interest in the drug business entirely, but only for a time.

Fourteen years later, on June 12, 1826, Joseph Charless,
retired printer, paid for an advertisement in the *Missouri
Republican*, successor to his own old *Missouri Gazette*,
announcing that

Joseph Charless, Sen. Main-Street, St. Louis, Begs leave to
inform his friends and the public, particularly practitioners
of Medicine, in Missouri and Illinois, that he has resumed his
former profession of Apothecary and Druggist; and having
made an arrangement with one of the most respectable Drug
establishments in Philadelphia, is enabled to offer for sale, on
very moderate terms, the following catalogue of genuine
Drugs, Medicines, Paints, &c.

He then itemized a wide variety of materials for sale. He
set up shop in a two-story white stone house at number
38, Main Street. Both the upper and lower stories of the
house contained two rooms, there was a broad porch
across the upper back of the house, and there was a de-
tached kitchen in the rear of the yard. From this stand
Charless sold all kinds of drugs, in addition to such other
commodities as garden seeds, paper, sealing wax, paint,
printing ink, alcohol, and sperm oil until his retirement

from that trade seven years later.

In 1828 Joseph Charless, junior, entered into partnership with his father in the drug firm, and thereafter it conducted business under the style "Jos. Charless & Son." [4] The firm prospered rapidly and soon became a very extensive operation. Some impression of the magnitude of their business may be deduced from an inventory of some of their stock published on January 10, 1832, when they announced their removal to a new location in the brick store "lately occupied by Robert Rankin, corner of Main and Pine Streets" nearly opposite their old stand.[5] It lists

1200 lbs.	Crude Arsenic, for Shot makers;
2240 lbs.	Crude Sulphur, for Powder makers;
500 gals.	Spirits Turpentine, and Linseed Oil;
4000 lbs.	Sal Aratus, Pearl and Pot Ashes;
2000 lbs.	Refined and Crude Salt Petre;
5000 lbs.	Ground and Stick Logwood;
3000 lbs.	Copperas, Alum, and Indigo;
12 casks	Fustic, Nicaraugua, camwood, Spanish Brown, Ven, Red, and yellow Ochre;
25 casks	Spanish White, Chalk, Rotten Stone, Pumice Stone, Stone Ochre, Red, White, and Black head, Lampblack, and Ivory Black;
10 bbls.	fresh cold pressed castor oil;

A folio list of their stock and its prices, issued on February 12, 1833, and preserved in the Missouri Historical Society, itemizes no fewer than 250 drugs and medicines for sale, in addition to such medical furnishings as catheters, lancets, needles, tourniquets, forceps, trocars, and galley pots. Not of least importance was their supply of paint, which was very extensive.

Charless and his son advertised their wares widely in many newspapers in Missouri and Illinois and the business was highly successful. In an article reviewing their work, published in the St. Louis *Globe-Democrat* on April 30, 1922, the importance of their firm was described in the following way: "Together they built it into one of the greatest drug houses in America. Charless made a fortune and helped to found the prestige St. Louis has always held as a drug market." No doubt the senior Charless enjoyed most the opportunity to develop a successful business in an atmosphere of political tranquility, an atmosphere that had been denied him as a publisher.

By the end of 1832 Charless, now over sixty years of age, decided to retire for a second time. His valedictory from the drug trade required much less space to print than his valedictory from printing twelve years earlier. It required a two-sentence paid advertisement in the *Missouri Republican* of January 1, 1833. "Notice is hereby given," it read, "that the firm of Jos. Charless & Son is this day dissolved by mutual consent. All persons having demands against said firm, will present them to Joseph Charless, Jr. for liquidation." Charless, *fils*, however, remained in the drug trade, and it continued to grow throughout his life.

During almost his entire stay in St. Louis the senior Charless had also been active investing, as it were, in the future of the town by buying and selling real estate. Earliest evidence of his interest in acquiring land in the territory lies in a letter from him to Pierre Chouteau, dated July 10, 1810,[6] which reads:

Since I had the pleasure of speaking to you on the subject of the two Arpents [7] of Land adjoining Mr. Carr's tract, I had a conversation with Mr. Bradberry, he considers the piece too small for him and has declined the purchase—Could you make the payments easy I would be glad to have it, in fact my business is such as to afford me leisure to attend the raising a support from a few acres of Land.

I would pay you the price you ask but would not be able to pay soon, for that reason I would be willing pay [sic] interest untill the whole is paid. I have on my book upwards of $1200 and I shall use every exertion to collect and pay.

It does not appear, however, that this piece of property ever came to belong to the printer; at any rate there is no record of its transfer at this time.

Charless' first major property transaction of record in St. Louis was his purchase on June 18, 1816, of "a piece of land upon the hill," from Auguste Chouteau for $740.[8] The "hill" was the high land a little to the west of St. Louis' growing business district, and it was to this area that the older, affluent residents of the city were repairing to build their more gracious and spacious, modern homes. Charless did not move immediately to the property, however. Instead, on November 9, 1816, he purchased from Abraham Gallatin for $1,000 a lot 60 x 100 feet on the southeast corner of Church and Walnut Streets.[9] It is reported that there was at the time a two-story frame house on this property in which the Charless family had already resided for some years and into which the printer now moved his printing office,[10] and in which he operated it for several years thereafter. It was not until early 1819 that the carpenter Robert Patton built for Charless a two-story brick building "on the hill" at the southeast corner of Fifth and Main Streets. Charless moved his family into the new home and offered to rent out his house on Church and Walnut, it "having a good dry cellar, store room, and two chambers on the second floor, kitchen,

&c." [11] Charless lived out his remaining fifteen years in his new house on the hill.

Many of Charless' subsequent real estate transactions were made for the specific benefit of his family. For some reason that is unclear he mortgaged his new home for $1,000 on September 22, 1821, and then sold it to his son Edward three days later for $4,000, only to buy it back again eighteen months after that for $3500, although he continued to live there throughout the period. It is probable that no money actually changed hands in this transaction but that it was rather designed to furnish Edward with collateral during his negotiations for the purchase of the proprietorship of the *Missouri Republican,* which took place during this period. On June 1, 1822, he also deeded over to his daughter Ann a piece of property, but this may have acted in effect as a dowry, since she had married a week earlier. On November 1, 1831, he purchased from William Clark for $5,136.67 the brick store on the corner of Pine and Main Streets into which he and his son removed their drug store nine weeks later. He later deeded this over to his son Joseph.[12] There were also other real estate transactions in St. Louis involving Charless during this period, and there is also evidence that he held other properties in the surrounding region, but these few are the most pertinent.

Charless' brick house on the hill was added to in 1820, making it an imposing structure that was referred to from that time until it was torn down almost a half century later as "the Charless Mansion." Attached to the house was an extensive garden and orchard, where the publisher-apothecary raised fruits, flowers, and all kinds of vegetables, as well as currants, gooseberries, and grapes. The botanist Henry Shaw has reportedly said of

Charless that he had "a fine taste for horticulture" and raised "the first cultivated grapes in St. Louis." [13] In 1824, however, Charless claimed to have "declined the cultivation of the grape" and was prepared to "dispose of about 100 vines which rooted last year, and 1000 slips," including cape, muscatel, and Madeira.[14] The Charless Mansion faced onto the St. Louis Public Square and it occupied, together with its gardens, stables, smokehouse, kitchen, and other grounds, much of the block bounded by Market and Walnut, Fourth and Fifth Streets. The eastern portion of the block was subsequently occupied by the First Presbyterian Church, its parsonage, and cemetery. Near the northwest corner of the Public Square stood "the jailor's daughter," a public pillory for floggings, as well as stocks for less serious crimes. South of the Charless property stood the old arsenal and one of the two-story round forts with portholes that had been built by the early French settlers as a citadel against Indian attacks.[15]

It was in this house on the corner of Fifth and Market that Joseph Charless conducted still another business: that of hosteler. It has been mentioned that he once proposed opening a coffee house in Louisville, and he and his wife Sarah had long taken boarders into their home, so "entertainment" was not a completely new idea to him. As early as April 19, 1810, he had advertised

The subscriber respectfully informs his friends and the public generally, that he receives *Boarders* by the *day, week or month. Travellers* and all those who may favor him with their company can be accommodated with as good fare as the town affords (*Liquors excepted*) on the most moderate terms. Joseph Charless. Stabling for 8 or 10 horses can be had.

From time to time thereafter he reminded his readers
of his interest in accommodating boarders, but it was not
until his house on the hill was completed, with its twelve
apartments, some of them large enough to dine very large
parties,[16] that he appears to have entered seriously into
that business.

On May 9, 1821, Charless advertised his boarding
house and livery stable in the *Gazette* and gave the terms
under which he would welcome "those Gentlemen who
visit St. Louis, and Travellers generally." His charges
were as follows:

Boarding and Lodging per week	$4.50
For boarding only	3.50
For less than a week, per meal	.25
Lodging per night	.25
Horses taken in, per month	10.00
per week	3.00
per day	.50

Seven months later he reduced his price for a night's
lodging to 12½¢ and announced that he had "taken the
whole range of brick buildings and devoted it to the
reception of those who prefer quiet." [17] In 1823 he reduced his rates still further.[18]

In those early years there was a post in front of his
house on Market Street at the top of which there was
a sign suspended from an iron arm. On both sides of the
sign were painted pictures of a farmer, with his shirt
sleeves rolled up, plowing with two horses, one a bay and
the other a gray, and contemporary accounts report that
it was "evident from the style of the representation that
the brightness of coloring [was] the chief merit of paint-
ing." There was subsequently a second sign placed

diagonally on a post on the corner of Fifth and Market so that it was easily seen from both streets. This second sign contained a picture of the Charless Mansion itself, above which was the word "Entertainment" and below which was inscribed "By Joseph Charless." [19]

"In those days," the report continues, "this tavern was an important place, and, according to all accounts, the cheer and accommodation were excellent." This is one of the very few contemporary accounts of Charless' personality, another early one being Scharf's statement that he "was a man full of all good qualities, honored and respected by all who knew him; simple in manner and habit, an impulsive, warm-hearted, generous Irishman, hospitable to a degree, and brimful of cheery humor." [20] Bradbury had referred to Charless in 1810 as a person "whose disposition and manners gain him the esteem of all who know him: mine he will always retain." [21] By far the most useful account, however, is that of Elihu Shepard, who, in mid-August of 1820, moved as a boarder into the newly opened "house of Mr. Joseph Charless, Sr., the most fashionable family in town, and whose dining room was a high school of etiquette and learning." He related that he met there several influential professional men and that

... these gentlemen and a few merchants of the town formed our family circle, together with Mr. Charless' two sons and two daughters.... He introduced me to his family and his boarders in such a manner that it put me at once quite on a par with any and all of them, and I was no longer a stranger in the family. The consequence was, that within the next two weeks I had been introduced to almost every prominent American in the town, and several of the French.[22]

Since this account concerns almost exactly the period in which Charless was retiring from his publishing business, it appears that he must have sustained a fair number of important friendships during the time. It also appears that he had the personal qualities essential to a successful inn-keeper.

On July 28, 1834, Joseph Charless died at his brick home on the hill. He was sixty-two years of age and had been successful in every kind of business venture he had attempted. He had been an editor, a bookseller, a publisher, an apothecary, a hosteler, and an entrepreneur, combining them all into his role as a pioneer. He would no doubt like to have been remembered primarily, however, for his work as a printer in the Western Country.

Appendix A

POSTLUDE: THE FAMILY

Joseph Charless had outlived most of the members of his family. His stepson Robert M'Cloud had been born in Philadelphia in 1795. Growing up in his step-father's offices, he became a journeyman printer and in 1820 established a newspaper of his own called the *Missourian*, in St. Charles, Missouri, twenty-five miles northeast of St. Louis. In 1827 he married Daphne S. Emmons of St. Charles and died on May 1, 1832, "after a severe illness of pulmonary consumption." [1]

Charless' own firstborn, Edward, had also grown up a journeyman printer in his father's offices. Eighteen months after his father's retirement from publishing, in March 1822, Edward took over the proprietorship of the *Missouri Gazette* from his father's successor, changed its name to the *Missouri Republican*, and operated it highly successfully until 1837. The *Republican* later became the St. Louis *Republic* which was published continuously until 1919. Edward married Jane Louise Stoddard, also of St. Charles, in March of 1823 and died in 1848.

Joseph's second son, John, who had been born in Philadelphia in 1801 was a sickly youth; he died in St. Louis on August 31, 1816. [2]

Joseph's next son, Joseph, junior, born in Lexington in 1804, was also trained as a printer but appears never to have seriously considered practicing the trade. He graduated from Transylvania University and read law under Francis Spalding, who was at that time one of the leading members of the bar of St. Louis. Joseph practiced law only a short time, then gave up the profession in 1828 to join his father in the drug business. He married Charlotte Taylor Blow of St. Louis on November 8, 1831. Joseph, junior, died tragically in 1859 when he was murdered on the street by a man against whom he had testified in court.

Ann Charless, born in Lexington in 1806, was a *femme fatale*. On May 26, 1822, she was married to the attorney Amos Wheeler, who had earlier been largely responsible for the establishment of Little Rock as the capital of Arkansas. Two weeks after the marriage her husband died.[3] Fifteen months later Ann remarried, this time to Charless Wahrendorff, to whom she bore a daughter. Wahrendorff, however, died in 1831, and fourteen months later the twice-widowed Ann married Beverly Allen. This time fate reversed itself, and two weeks after her third marriage on November 1, 1832, Ann Charless Wheeler Wahrendorff Allen died while on her honeymoon in New Orleans.

Ann's younger sister Eliza, who had been born at Louisville the year her father was establishing his press in St. Louis, led a less exciting life. She married John Kerr in 1827 and died five years later.

Their mother, Joseph's wife, Sarah Jordan M'Cloud Charless, outlived her entire family but one, dying in St. Louis in 1852 at the age of eighty-one.

Appendix B

A LIST OF CHARLESS IMPRINTS

NEWSPAPERS AND MAGAZINES
   Mifflin Gazette, Lewistown, Pa., 1795-1796.
   Weekly Magazine, Philadelphia, Pa., 1799.
   Independent Gazetteer, Lexington, Ky., 1803.
   Louisville Gazette, Louisville, Ky., 1807-1809.
   Missouri Gazette [and *Louisiana Gazette*] St. Louis, Mo., 1808-1820.
BOOKS AND PAMPHLETS, OF WHICH COPIES ARE KNOWN TO EXIST
   Dibdin, Charles. *Dibdin's Museum, Being a Collection of the Newest and Most Admired Songs.* Philadelphia: Printed by R. Aitken, No. 22, Market-Street. For Joseph Charles, 1797. 72 p.
   Choice Tales; Consisting of an Elegant Collection of Delightful Little Pieces for the Instruction & Amusement of Young Persons. Philadelphia: Printed by Joseph Charless, for Mathew Carey, No. 118, Market Street, 1800. 170 p.
   [Condie, Thomas] *Biographical Memoirs of the Illustrious Gen. Geo: Washington....* Philadelphia: Printed by Charless & Ralston, 1800. 232 p.
   [Dodsley, Robert] *The Economy of Human Life....* Philadelphia: Printed by Charles & Ralston, for the Booksellers, 1800. 156 p.
   [Murdock, John] *The Beau Metamorphized, or The Generous Maid....* Philadelphia: Printed by Joseph C. Charless for the Author, 1800. 52 p.
   Bible. *The Holy Bible.... First Philadelphia Edition.* Philadelphia: Printed by Joseph Charless, for Mathew Carey, 1801. Unpaged.
   Bible. *The Holy Bible, Containing the Old and New Testaments, Together with the Apocrypha....* Philadelphia: Printed by Joseph Charless, for Mathew Carey, 1801. Unpaged.

138

Colman, George. *The Poor Gentleman.... Third Edition.* Philadelphia: Printed by J. Charless for P. Byrne, 1801. 75 p.

The Conductor Generalis, or The Office, Duty, and Authority of Justices of the Peace.... Philadelphia: Printed by Joseph Charless for Mathew Carey, 1801. 480 p.

Corry, John. *The Life of George Washington....* Philadelphia: Printed by Joseph Charless, for H. & P. Rice, 1801. 204 p.

Great Britain. Court of Chancery. *Reports of Cases Argued and Determined in the High Court of Chancery....* By Francis Vesey, Jun. Philadelphia: P. Byrne [Printed by Joseph Charless] 1802 v. I[?]–IV.

Great Britain. Court of King's Bench. *Reports of Cases Argued and Determined in the Court of King's Bench....* By Edward Hyde East ... Philadelphia: P. Byrne [Printed by Joseph Charless] 1802. v. II.

Rippon, John. A Selection of Hymns from the Best Authors.... Philadelphia: J. Charless, 1802. 621 p.

The Union Primer; or, An Easy Introduction to Reading and Spelling. Philadelphia: Joseph Charless, 1802.

Webster, Noah. *The Prompter....* Philadelphia: Printed by Joseph Charless, 1802. 80 p.

Baptists. Kentucky. Elkhorn Association. *Minutes of the Elkhorn Association of Baptists, Met at Town Fork Meeting-House, on Saturday the 13th Day of August, 1803.* [Lexington: Charless & Kay, 1803] 4 p.

Baptists. Kentucky. Green River Association. *Minutes of the Green River Association of Baptists, Met at Mount Gilead Meeting-House, in Green County, on Saturday the 23rd Day of July, 1803.* [Lexington: Joseph Charless, 1803] 4 p.

Charless' Kentucky, Tennessee & Ohio Almanac, for the Year of Our Lord 1804.... Lexington: Printed and Sold by Joseph Charless, 1803. 36 p.

Edwards, Jonathan. *Some Thoughts Concerning the Present Revival of Religion in New-England....* Lexington: Reprinted by Joseph Charless, from a Boston Edition Printed in the Year 1742, 1803. 412 p.

Hymns and Spiritual Songs, for the Use of Christians.... Lexington: Printed and Sold by Joseph Charless, Bookseller and Stationer, 1803. 246 p.

Presbyterian Church. Synod of Kentucky. *A Circular Letter from the Synod of Kentucky, to the Churches under Their Care.* Lexington: Printed by Joseph Charless, 1803. 36 p.

Rice, David. *A Sermon on the Present Revival of Religion, &c. in This Country....* Published at the Unanimous Request of the Synod. Lexington: Printed by Joseph Charless, 1803. 52 p.

A Selection of Hymns and Spiritual Songs, from the Best Authors.... Lexington: Printed by J. Charless, 1803. 331 p.

An Address to the Different Religious Societies, on the Sacred Import of the Christian Name. Lexington: Printed by Joseph Charless, 1804. 31 p.

Baptists. Kentucky. Elkhorn Association. *Minutes of the Elkhorn Association of Baptists, Met at North Elkhorn, 2nd Saturday in August, 1804.* [Lexington: Joseph Charless, 1804] 5 p.

Blythe, James. *The Death of the Good Man Precious in the Sight of God....* Lexington: Printed by Joseph Charless, 1804. 28 p.

Edwards, Peter. *Candid Reasons for Renouncing the Principles of Antipaedobaptism....* Fifth American Edition. Lexington: Printed by Joseph Charless, 1804. 124 p.

Guthrie, Jesse. *The American School-Master's Assistant; Being a Compendious System of Vulgar and Decimal Arithmetic....* Lexington: Printed and Sold by Joseph Charless, and by All the Store Keepers, 1804. 231 p.

The Importance of Family-Religion Stated and Enforced. Lexington: Printed by Joseph Charless, [1804?] 36 p.

[Macgowen, John] *Infernal Conference; or, Dialogues of Devils....* Lexington: Printed by Joseph Charless, [1804] 366 p.

Marshall, Walter. *The Gospel-Mystery of Sanctification Opened, in Sundry Practical Directions....* Lexington: Printed by Joseph Charless, and Sold at His Book-Store, Where May Be Had a Great Variety of Books on Different Subjects, 1804. 287 p.

Stone, Barton Warren. *An Apology for Renouncing the Jurisdiction of the Synod of Kentucky....* Lexington: Printed by Joseph Charless, January 31st, 1804. 141 p.

Taylor, Caleb Jarvis. *Spiritual Songs.* Lexington: Printed by Joseph Charless, Main Street, January 24, 1804. 30 p.

Two Letters Written by a Gentlemen [sic] *to His Friend in Kentucky....* Lexington: Printed by Joseph Charless [1804] 68 p.

Charless' Kentucky, Tennessee & Ohio Almanac, for the Year of Our Lord 1805.... Lexington: Printed and Sold by Joseph Charless, At His Book-Printing Office, 1805. 36 p.

Charless' Kentucky, Tennessee and Ohio Almanac for the Year 1806.... Lexington: Printed by Joseph Charless, Who Has

on Hand a Variety of School Books, &c. Which He Will Sell,
by Wholesale, at Philadelphia Prices, without Carriage [1805]
26 p.

Dow, Lorenzo. *The Chain of Lorenzo.* . . . Lexington: Printed
by Joseph Charless, Main Street, 1805. 52 p.

Edwards, Peter. *Renouncing Antipaedobaptism.* . . . Sixth American Edition. Lexington: Printed by Joseph Charless, 1805.
124 p.

Head, Jesse. *A Reply to the Arguments Advanced by the Rev.
Thomas Cleland.* . . . Lexington: Printed by Joseph Charless,
1805. 60 p.

*Hints for the Consideration of the Friends of Slavery, and
Friends of Emancipation.* . . . Lexington: Printed by Joseph
Charless, 1805. 32 p.

Kelburn, Sinclare. *The Divinity of Our Lord Jesus Christ, As-
serted and Proved.* . . . Lexington: Printed by Joseph Charless,
in Main-Street, 1805. 66 p.

Ohio. General Assembly. House of Representatives. *Journal.* . . .
Being the First Session of the Third General Assembly. . . .
Vol. III. Published by Authority. Lexington: Printed by
Joseph Charless, for N. Willis, 1805. 175 p.

Sabin, Elijah R. *A Discourse on Gospel Discipline. In Three
Parts.* Lexington: Printed by Joseph Charless, 1805. 51 p.

Stone, Barton Warren. *Atonement.* . . . Lexington: Printed by
Joseph Charless, Main Street, 1805. 36 p.

Stone, Barton Warren. *A Reply to John P. Campbell's Strictures
on Atonement.* Lexington: Printed by Joseph Charless, 1805.
67 p.

*Charless' Kentucky, Tennessee, and Ohio Almanac for the Year
1807.* . . . Lexington: Printed by Joseph Charless, Who Has
on Hand a Variety of School Books, &c. Which He Will Sell,
by Wholesale, at Philadelphia Prices [1806] 36 p.

Lenglet du Fresnoy, Nicolas. *Geography for Children; or, A
Short and Easy Method of Teaching and Learning Geog-
raphy.* . . . Lexington: Reprinted and Published by Joseph
Charless, 1806. 156 p.

*Useful Discovery in a Letter Addressed to the Rev. Mr. C*****
and Mr. M*** I Never Saw the Like Before.* [Lexington:
Printed by Joseph Charless] 1806. 12 p.

*The American Orator: Containing Rules and Directions, Cal-
culated to Improve Youth and Others in the Ornamental
and Useful Art of Eloquence.* Lexington: Printed and Sold

by Joseph Charless, and by All the Merchants in the Western Country, 1807. 300 p.

The Kentucky Almanack, for the Year of Our Lord 1808. . . . Lexington: Printed for Joseph Charless [1807] 36 p.

Bates, Frederick. *An Oration, Delivered before Saint Louis Lodge, No. 111. . . . on Wednesday the 9th Day of November, 1808.* Saint Louis: Printed by Joseph Charless, 1809. 19 p.

Louisiana (Territory) Laws, Statutes, etc. *The Laws of the Territory of Louisiana. Comprising All Those Which Are Now Actually in Force within the Same.* Published by Authority. St. Louis: Printed by Joseph Charless, Printer to the Territory, 1808 [*i.e.,* 1809] 376, [58] p.

Louisiana (Territory) Laws, Statutes, etc. *Laws of the Territory of Louisiana: Passed by the Governor and Judges Assembled in Legislature, in the Month of October, 1810.* Published by Authority. St. Louis: Printed by Joseph Charless, Printer to the Territory, 1810. 39 p.

Missouri Fur Company, St. Louis. *Articles of Association.* [St. Louis: Printed by Joseph Charless, 1812] Broadside.

Lucas, John B. C. *To the Public.* [St. Louis: Printed by Joseph Charless, 1814] Broadside.

Missouri (Territory) Laws, Statutes, etc. *Acts Passed by the General Assembly, of the Territory of Missouri; in July and August, One Thousand Eight Hundred and Thirteen.* St. Louis: Printed by Joseph Charless. Printer to the Territory, 1813 [*i.e.,* 1814] 95 p.

Missouri (Territory) Laws, Statutes, etc. *Acts Passed by the General Assembly of the Territory of Missouri: in December and January, One Thousand Eight Hundred and Thirteen and Fourteen.* St. Louis: Printed by Joseph Charless, Printer to the Territory, 1814. ʻ108 p.

Missouri (Territory) Laws, Statutes, etc. *Acts Passed by the General Assembly, of the Territory of Missouri; in December and January, One Thousand Eight Hundred and Fourteen and Fifteen.* St. Louis: Printed by Joseph Charless, Printer to the Territory, 1815. 164 p.

Lucas, Charles. *To the People of Missouri Territory. Charles Lucas' Exposition of a Late Difference between John Scott and Himself.* St. Louis: Printed at the Missouri Gazette Office, 1816. 24 p.

Missouri (Territory) Laws, Statutes, etc. *Acts Passed by the General Assembly of the Territory of Missouri; in December and January, One Thousand Eight Hundred and Fifteen and Sixteen.* St. Louis: Printed by Joseph Charless, Printer to the Territory, 1816. 143 p.

Charless' Missouri & Illinois Magazine Almanac, for 1818.... St. Louis: Printed and Sold by Joseph Charless; Where Printing of Every Description is Executed Expeditiously, and on the Most Reasonable Terms [1817] 62 p.

Missouri (Territory) Laws, Statutes, etc. *Acts Passed by the General Assembly of the Territory of Missouri; in December and January, One Thousand Eight Hundred and Sixteen and Seventeen.* St. Louis: Printed by Joseph Charless. Printer to the Territory, 1817. 140 p.

Geyer, Henry S. *A Digest of the Laws of Missouri Territory....* St. Louis: Printed for the Publisher, by Joseph Charless, at the Missouri Gazette Office, 1818. 486, xxvi, [30] p.

Missouri (Territory) Laws, Statutes, etc. *Acts Passed by the General Assembly of the Territory of Missouri, in October, November and December, One Thousand Eight Hundred and Eighteen.* St. Louis: Printed by Joseph Charless, Printer to the Territory, 1819. 160 p.

[Beck, Abraham] *Western Land Agency and Commission Office.* [St. Louis: Jos. Charless, Printer, 1820] 32 p.

Missouri. Constitution. *Constitution de l'état du Missouri.* [St. Louis: Joseph Charless, 1820] 24 p.

United Society for the Spread of the Gospel. *Report of the Board of Managers ... at Their First Annual Meeting Held at Looking Glass Prairie, Madison Co. Illinois, October 9th, 1819.* St. Louis: Printed by Joseph Charless, 1820. 8 p.

ADDITIONAL TITLES REPORTED TO HAVE BEEN PRINTED BY CHARLESS BUT OF WHICH NO COPIES ARE RECORDED

Goody Two Shoes. Philadelphia: Printed by Joseph Charless for Mathew Carey, 1800.

Little Boy Found Under a Haycock. Philadelphia: Printed by Joseph Charless for Mathew Carey, 1800.

Little Francis. Philadelphia: Printed by Joseph Charless for Mathew Carey, 1800.

Tommy Two Shoes. Philadelphia: Printed by Joseph Charless for Mathew Carey, 1800.

Giant Grumbo. Philadelphia: Printed by Joseph Charless for Mathew Carey, 1801.

Many Boys and Girls. Philadelphia: Printed by Joseph Charless for Mathew Carey. 1801.

Whittington and His Cat. Philadelphia: Printed by Joseph Charless for Mathew Carey, 1801.

An Answer to the Apology of the Springfield Presbytery. Lexington: Joseph Charless, 1804.

Bingham, Caleb. *The American Preceptor. A Selection of Lessons for Reading and Speaking. Designed for the Use of Schools.* Lexington: Printed by Joseph Charless, 1805.

Harrison, Ralph. *English Grammar.* Lexington: Joseph Charless, 1806.

Murray, Lindley. *English Grammar.* Lexington: Joseph Charless, 1806.

The Union Primer. Lexington: Joseph Charless, 1806.

Webster, Noah. *The Promptor.* Lexington: Joseph Charless, 1806.

Webster, Noah. *Webster's Spelling Book.* Lexington: Joseph Charless, 1806.

Louisiana (Territory) Laws, Statutes, etc. *An Act Regulating the Fiscal Concerns of the Territory, Defining the Duties of Certain Officers Concerned Therewith, and For Other Purposes.* St. Louis: Joseph Charless, 1808.

Missouri (Territory) Laws, Statutes, etc. *An Act Supplementary to an Act to Reduce into One the Several Laws Regulating the Militia.* St. Louis: Joseph Charless, 1816.

NOTES

CHAPTER I

1. *Missouri Republican,* June 12, 1826.
2. *Deed Books,* v. 454, p. 574, Memorial no. 304960.
3. This book, together with other records of the guild, is in the possession of Messrs. H. Sibthorpe & Son, 33 Molesworth Street, Dublin.
4. E. R. McC. Dix, "Printing in Mullingar," *Irish Book Lover* 2 (1911) 120-122.
5. Douglas C. McMurtrie, *Joseph Charless, Pioneer Printer of St. Louis* (Chicago, Ludlow Typograph Co., 1931) p. 13.

CHAPTER II

1. *Missouri Gazette,* October 25, 1817.
2. *Ibid.,* July 13, 1816.
3. Except where otherwise noted, all letters referred to in this work are among the Carey papers in the Historical Society of Pennsylvania.
4. Mathew Carey, *Autobiography* (Brooklyn, Schwaab, 1942) pp. 10, 20. For best accounts of Mathew Carey, see his autobiography and Earl L. Bradsher's *Mathew Carey, Editor, Author and Publisher* (N.Y., Columbia University Press, 1912).
5. See, for example, David Kaser, "Retirement Income of Mathew Carey," *Pennsylvania Magazine of History and Biography* 70 (1956) 410-15.
6. January 5, 1796. The Carey Letter Books are also preserved in the Historical Society of Pennsylvania.
7. There was in 1796 a Michael Duffey printing at 48 High Street in Philadelphia. It may have been he who purchased Charless' office, for in that year he disappeared from Philadelphia, although he probably reappeared there as a printer

145

between 1803 and 1820, spelling his name Michael Duffie.

8. Robert Aitken (1734-1802), bookseller, was a Scots Quaker who emigrated to Philadelphia and printed there the first American Bible in English in 1782.

9. Letter from Charless to James Monroe, February 7, 1813, published in U.S. Dept. of State, *Territorial Papers of the United States*, ed. by Clarence E. Carter (Washington, Government Printing Office, 1949) XIV, 629.

10. See, for example, William Hyde and Howard L. Conard, eds., *Encyclopedia of the History of St. Louis*, 4 vols. (N.Y. Southern History Co., 1899) I, 350.

11. John T. Scharf, *History of St. Louis City and County*, 2 vols. (Philadelphia, Everts, 1883) II, 903.

12. "Records of Pennsylvania Marriages Prior to 1810," *Pennsylvania Archives*, 2d Ser., v. 9 (Harrisburg, Hart, 1880) II, 576.

13. *New Trade Directory for Philadelphia Anno 1800* (Philadelphia, Way & Groff, 1799).

14. Leila Crawford, "A Checklist of Gettysburg, Pennsylvania Imprints for the Years 1801-76," (Unpub. M.S. thesis, Catholic University of America, 1960) p. 21.

15. "The Early Career of Joseph Charless, the First Printer in Missouri," *Missouri Historical Review* 26 (1932) 342-53.

16. Hugh Gaine was himself an Irish immigrant from Belfast who had come to America in 1745 and had become one of the important colonial printers. He gave up active printing in 1800 but continued bookselling in New York until his death in 1807.

17. Margaret T. Hills, *The English Bible in America* (N.Y., American Bible Society, 1961) p. xvii.

18. Mathew Carey, *op. cit.*, p. 47.

19. Thomas Wall, *The Sign of Dr. Hay's Head* (Dublin, Gill, 1958) p. 39.

20. Hyde and Conard, *op. cit.*, I, 350.

21. "Early Career . . . ," p. 350.

CHAPTER III

1. See, for example, John Bradbury, *Travels in the Interior of America* (Cleveland, Arthur C. Clark, 1904) pp. 300-302; F. A. Michaux, *Travels to the West of the Alleghany Mountains* (London, Crosby, 1805) pp. 71-72; and Francis Baily, *Journal of a Tour in Unsettled Parts of North America* (London, Baily, 1856) pp. 146-47.

2. This extensive mercantile firm had been established in Lexington in 1793 by the father of Samuel and George Trotter. It continued until 1833.
3. Letter from Charless to Carey, June 27, 1803.
4. Letter from Charless to Carey, January 13, 1803.
5. Michaux, *op. cit.*, pp. 122-23.
6. J. Winston Coleman, Jr., *Lexington's First City Directory* (Lexington, Winburn Press, 1953) p. 3.
7. Letter from Charless to Carey, February 22, 1803.
8. *Kentucky Gazette*, August 16, 1803.
9. Announcements in the *Kentucky Gazette* of the dates indicated.
10. William Leavy, "Memoir of Lexington and Its Vicinity With Some Notice of Any Prominent Citizens...," *Kentucky Historical Society Register* 41 (1943) 320.
11. Letter from Charless to Carey, November 7, 1803.
12. Letter from Charless to Carey, March 22, 1803.
13. Part of the imprint in *Charless' Kentucky, Tennessee & Ohio Almanac* for 1804.
14. Colophon in Charless' 1803 edition of Edwards' *Some Thoughts Concerning the Present Revival of Religion.*
15. Letter from Charless to Carey, September 20, 1803.
16. Lawrence Wroth, *Parson Weems* (Baltimore, Eichelberger, 1911) *passim.*, and David Kaser, *Messrs. Carey & Lea of Philadelphia* (Philadelphia, University of Pennsylvania Press, 1957) pp. 30-34.
17. Letters from Charless to Carey, September 12 and November 5, 1805.
18. Frank Luther Mott, *Golden Multitudes, the Story of Best Sellers in the United States,* (N.Y., Macmillan, 1947) p. 299.
19. Henry Clay, *Papers,* ed. by James F. Hopkins (Lexington, University of Kentucky Press, 1959) I, 254.
20. Fayette County, Kentucky, Circuit Court, *Deed Books,* No. C, p. 201, February 23, 1807.
21. Kentucky, House of Representatives, *Journal,* 1805, p. 104.
22. Fayette County, Kentucky, County Court, *Order Book,* No. 1, p. 379, May 12, 1806.
23. Fayette County, Kentucky, County Court, *Deed Book,* No. C, p. 171, October 4, 1807.
24. Letter to Charless from Frederick Bates in Bates, *Life and Papers,* 2 vols., ed. by Thomas Maitland Marshall (St. Louis, Missouri Historical Society, 1926) I, 309-10.
25. Clay, *op. cit.*, I, 327.

CHAPTER IV

1. *Territorial Papers*, XIII, 196.
2. *Kentucky Gazette*, September 24, 1805.
3. This letter is preserved among the Clark Mss. in the Missouri Historical Society and is quoted here from the article by Roy T. King, "The Territorial Press in Missouri," *Missouri Historical Society Bulletin* 11 (1954) 73-81. This article also contains several other anecdotes from Charless' life.
4. *Missouri Republican*, Annual Review, 1854.
5. Charles van Ravenswaay, "Pioneer Presses in Missouri," *Missouri Historical Society Bulletin* 7 (1951) 296-301. The Farrar Mss. Account Books are in the Missouri Historical Society.
6. This prospectus is preserved in the Missouri Historical Society and is reprinted here from McMurtrie's pamphlet, *Joseph Charless*, pp. 20-22. Several other anecdotes concerning Charless' experiences in St. Louis are recorded in this useful booklet.
7. Henry Marie Brackenridge, *Views of Louisiana* (Pittsburgh, Cramer, Spear and Eichbaum, 1814) pp. 120-24.
8. van Ravenswaay, *op. cit.*, p. 298.
9. Isaiah Thomas, *History of Printing in America*, 2 vols. (Albany, Munsell, 1874) I, 36 n.
10. For a history of these reprints see *Missouri Historical Review* 32 (1938) 395-97.
11. *Territorial Papers*, XIV, 299 n.
12. Meriwether Lewis manuscript account book, which is preserved in the Missouri Historical Society.
13. January 4, April 5, 1809.
14. Much of the material presented here concerning the first book printed west of the Mississippi has already appeared, almost verbatim, in the author's "First Trans-Mississippi Imprint," *Papers of the Bibliographical Society of America* 52 (1958) 306-309, and is printed here with the permission of the editors.
15. Historical Records Survey, *Preliminary Check List of Missouri Imprints, 1808-1850* (Washington, 1937) p. 5.
16. Apparently there was some question in the minds of Missouri officials concerning the appropriate source of Charless' reimbursement as Printer to the Territory. See letter from Frederick Bates to Albert Gallatin, dated July 16, 1809, in the former's *Life and Papers*, II, 73.

17. *Missouri Gazette*, September 27, 1810.
18. Bates, *op. cit.*, II, 166-67.
19. *Territorial Papers*, XIV, 455.
20. Walter B. Stevens, *St. Louis, the Fourth City, 1764-1909* (St. Louis, Clarke, 1909) p. 196.
21. *Joseph Charless*, p. 30.
22. *Op. cit.*, p. 89.
23. William Roscoe Papers, No. 782. These letters are preserved in the Liverpool Public Library.

CHAPTER V

1. *Missouri Gazette*, January 25, February 1, 1809.
2. *Ibid.*, September 13, 1809; April 26, 1810.
3. *Territorial Papers*, XV, 222.
4. Bailey E. Birkhead, "A Study of the Missouri Gazette through the Editorship of Its Founder, Joseph Charless," (Unpub. M.A. Thesis, University of Missouri, 1945) p. 7.
5. King, *op. cit.*, p. 75.
6. *Missouri Gazette*, October 31, 1812.
7. *Ibid.*, January 22, 1814.
8. *Ibid.*, August 15, 1812.
9. *Ibid.*, October 12, 1816.
10. *Ibid.*, July 26, 1809; December 19, 1810; June 6, 1812.
11. *Ibid.*, August 16, 1809; July 23, 1814; January 9, 1811; November 9, 1809; March 28, August 15, 1812; January 9, 1813; October 14, 1815, respectively.
12. *Ibid.*, June 17, 1815.
13. *Ibid.*, November 23, 1809.
14. *Op. cit.*, p. 50.
15. For a good account of these activities, see Eugene M. Violette, "Spanish Land Claims in Missouri," *Washington University Studies* 8 (1921), Humanistic Series, No. 2, 167-200.
16. *Missouri Gazette*, January 4, 1809.

CHAPTER VI

1. Much of the material in the ensuing paragraphs was presented in a paper read by the author before the Bibliographical Society of America, meeting in Cleveland, Ohio, on July 10, 1961.
2. February 7, 1813, *Territorial Papers*, XIV, 630-31.

3. *Missouri Gazette,* September 12, 1812.
4. *Ibid.,* February 5, 1814.
5. Benjamin Howard had been born in Virginia but had spent most of his life in Kentucky. After serving in Congress he was appointed Territorial Governor of Missouri, but in March 1813 he resigned the governorship to accept a commission as brigadier general. Assigned to the Eighth Military District, which embraced the territory west of the Mississippi, General Howard's military service was limited to some Indian skirmishes. He died in St. Louis before the end of the war.
6. *Ibid.,* February 12, 1814.
7. *Territorial Papers,* XIV, 221, 293-312.
8. *Missouri Gazette,* July 16, 1814.
9. *Ibid.,* April 30, 1814.
10. *Ibid.,* November 12, 1814.
11. *Ibid.,* January 25, 1815.
12. This letter, although inscribed April 16, 1817, was probably meant to have been dated April 16, 1815. It is quoted here from Ninian Edwards, *The Edwards Papers,* ed, by E. B. Washburne (Chicago, Fergus, 1884) pp. 133-34.
13. *Missouri Gazette,* September 6, 1817.
14. *Territorial Papers,* XV, 341.
15. *Missouri Gazette,* September 6, 1817.

CHAPTER VII

1. Dated April 29, 1819, this letter is in the New-York Historical Society.
2. In a letter dated May 2, 1819, preserved among the Carey papers in the Historical Society of Pennsylvania.
3. *Missouri Gazette,* October 20, 1819.
4. *Ibid.,* April 12, 1820.
5. St. Louis *Enquirer,* April 15, 1820.
6. For further information, see Benjamin Merkel, *The Anti-slavery Controversy in Missouri, 1819-1865,* (Ph.D. diss., Washington University, 1939), *passim.*
7. *Missouri Gazette,* May 10, 1820.
8. Both of these accounts were noted in the St. Louis *Enquirer,* July 26, August 2, 1820.
9. Arthur J. Stansbury, *Report of the Trial of James H. Peck* (Boston, Hilliard Gray, 1833) p. 353.
10. Missouri, House of Representatives, *Journal.* 1st General Assembly, 1st Session, pp. 66, 89-90.

11. Meriwether Lewis and Benjamin Howard.
12. William Clark had been appointed governor of the Missouri Territory in 1813 and was at this time being discussed as a possible gubernatorial candidate for the new state.
13. Benton was later in 1820 elected to the U.S. Senate where he served for a quarter-century.
14. When Illinois became a state in 1818, Territorial Governor Ninian Edwards became its first U.S. Senator.
15. Isaac N. Henry, although a young man, died four months later.
16. Duff Green was an influential member of both the Missouri constitutional convention and the subsequent state legislature; Jonathan S. Findley, quondam schoolteacher from Pennsylvania, was also a member of the constitutional convention.

CHAPTER VIII

1. Letters dated April 18, 1812; January 3, 1813; in Ninian Edwards, *The Edwards Papers* (Chicago, Fergus, 1884) pp. 68, 91-93.
2. *Territorial Papers*, XV, 48-49.
3. *Ibid.*, 341.
4. *Ibid.*, 338-39.
6. U.S. *Statutes at Large* (Boston, Little & Brown, 1846) III, 439.
7. Missouri Territory, House of Representatives, *Journal,* January 14, 1815.
8. *Ibid.*, January 16, 1816.
9. *Missouri Gazette*, December 14, 1816.
10. *Ibid.*, August 2, 1820.
11. August 12, 1820.

CHAPTER IX

1. Letter from Charless to Chouteau, July 10, 1810, preserved in the Missouri Historical Society.
2. *Missouri Gazette*, July 29, 1815; January 6, 1816.
3. *Ibid.*, July 11, 1812.
4. *Ibid.*, November 4, 1828.
5. *Ibid.*, January 24, 31, 1832.
6. Preserved in the Missouri Historical Society.
7. The *arpent de Paris,* which was used for land grants in Missouri, amounted to .84 acre.

8. St. Louis *Deed Books*, G, 378.
9. *Ibid.*, F, 112.
10. Scharf, *op. cit.*, I, 903.
11. *Missouri Gazette*, April 21, 1819.
12. St. Louis *Deed Books*, K, 387; K, 351; L, 275; L, 86; R, 485; S, 320, respectively.
13. King, *op. cit.*, 78.
14. *Missouri Republican*, March 15, 1824.
15. *Ibid.*, January 21, 1868.
16. *Missouri Gazette*, July 26, 1820.
17. *Ibid.*, December 12, 1821.
18. *Missouri Republican*, January 25, 1823.
19. *Ibid.*, January 21, 1868.
20. Scharf, *op. cit.*, II, 1391.
21. Bradbury, *op. cit.*, p. 198.
22. *Autobiography* (St. Louis, Knapp, 1869) pp. 90-91.

APPENDIX A

1. van Ravenswaay, *op. cit.*, p. 299.
2. *Missouri Gazette*, September 7, 1816.
3. Stephen Hempstead, Sr., "I At Home," *Missouri Historical Society Bulletin* 15 (1959) 233.

SOURCES CONSULTED

Mathew Carey Account Books, in the American Antiquarian Society.

Mathew Carey Papers, in the Historical Society of Pennsylvania.

Draper MSS, in the State Historical Society of Wisconsin.

Dublin, Corporation of Cutlers, Painters, Paperstainers, and Stationers (Guild of St. Luke), Records and Accounts, in the possession of Messrs. H. Sibthorpe & Son, 33 Molesworth Street, Dublin.

Dublin, Registry of Deeds, Deeds.

Farrar Manuscript Account Books, in the Missouri Historical Society.

Fayette County, Kentucky, Circuit Court, Deeds.

Killucan Parish, County Westmeath, Registers.

Meriwether Lewis Account Book, in the Missouri Historical Society.

William Roscoe Papers, in the Liverpool Public Library.

St. Louis, Missouri, Recorder of Deeds, Deeds.

John W. Taylor Papers, in the New-York Historical Society.

NEWSPAPERS

Independent Gazetteer
Kentucky Gazette
Louisville Gazette
Missouri Gazette
Missouri Republican
St. Louis Enquirer

BOOKS AND ARTICLES

BAILY, FRANCIS. *Journal of a Tour in Unsettled Parts of North America.* London: Baily, 1856.

BATES, FREDERICK. *Life and Papers.* St. Louis: Missouri Historical Society, 1926. 2 vols.

BILLON, FREDERIC L. *Annals of St. Louis in Its Territorial Days.* St. Louis: Printed for the Author, 1888.

BIRKHEAD, BAILY E. "A Study of the Missouri Gazette Through the Editorship of Its Founder, Joseph Charless" (Unpub. M.A. thesis, University of Missouri, 1945).

BRACKENRIDGE, HENRY MARIE. *Views of Louisiana.* Pittsburgh: Cramer, Spear and Eichbaum, 1814.

BRADBURY, JOHN. *Travels in the Interior of America.* Cleveland: Arthur H. Clark Co., 1904.

BRADSHER, EARL. *Mathew Carey, Editor, Author and Publisher.* New York: Columbia University Press, 1912.

BROWN, H. GLENN, and BROWN, MAUDE O. *A directory of the Book-Arts and Book Trade in Philadelphia to 1820.* New York: New York Public Library, 1950.

CAREY, MATHEW. *Autobiography.* Brooklyn: Schwaab, 1942.

CHAMBERS, WILLIAM N. *Old Bullion Benton.* Boston: Little, Brown & Co., 1956.

CLAY, HENRY. *Papers.* Lexington: University of Kentucky Press, 1959-   . v. 1- .

COLEMAN, J. WINSTON. *Lexington's First City Directory.* Lexington: Winburn Press, 1953.

CRAWFORD, LEILA. "A Checklist of Gettysburg, Pennsylvania Imprints for the Years 1801-76," (Unpub. M.S. thesis, Catholic University of America, 1960).

DIX, E. R. McC. "Printing in Mullingar," *Irish Book Lover* 2 (1911) 120-22.

EDWARDS, NINIAN. *The Edwards Papers.* Chicago: Fergus, 1884. (Chicago Historical Society's Collection, v. 3).

HANNA, CHARLES A. *The Wilderness Trail.* New York: Putnam, 1911. 2 vols.

HEMPSTEAD, STEPHEN, SR. "I At Home," *Missouri Historical*

Society Bulletin 13 (1956-57) 30-56, 283-317; 14 (1957-58) 59-96, 272-88; 15 (1958-59) 33-48, 224-47.

HILLS, MARGARET T. *The English Bible in America.* New York: American Bible Society, 1961.

HISTORICAL RECORDS SURVEY. *Preliminary Check List of Missouri Imprints, 1808-1850.* Washington, 1937.

HYDE, WILLIAM, and CONARD, HOWARD L. *Encyclopedia of the History of St. Louis.* New York: Southern History Co., 1899. 4 vols.

JENNINGS, SISTER MARIETTA. *A Pioneer Merchant of St. Louis, 1810-1820.* New York: Columbia University Press, 1939.

KASER, DAVID. *A Directory of the St. Louis Book and Printing Trades to 1850.* New York: New York Public Library, 1961.

————. "The First Trans-Mississippi Imprint," *Papers of the Bibliographical Society of America* 52 (1958) 306-09.

————. *Messrs. Carey & Lea of Philadelphia.* Philadelphia: University of Pennsylvania Press, 1957.

————. "Retirement Income of Mathew Carey," *Pennsylvania Magazine of History and Biography* 70 (1956) 410-15.

KING, ROY T. "The Territorial Press in Missouri," *Missouri Historical Society Bulletin* 11 (1954) 73-81.

LEAVY, WILLIAM. "Memoir of Lexington and Its Vicinity," *Kentucky State Historical Society Register* 40 (1942) 107-31, 253-67, 353-75; 41 (1943) 44-62, 107-37, 250-60, 310-46; 42 (1944) 26-53.

LYONS, WILLIAM HENRY. *The Pioneer Editor in Missouri.* (Ph.D. diss., University of Missouri, 1958).

McMURTRIE, DOUGLAS C. *Checklist of Kentucky Imprints, 1787-1810.* Louisville: Historical Records Survey, 1939.

————. "The Early Career of Joseph Charless, the First Printer in Missouri," *Missouri Historical Review* 26 (1932) 342-53.

————. *Joseph Charless; Pioneer Printer of St. Louis.* Chicago: Ludlow Typograph Co., 1931.

————. "A Supplementary List of Kentucky Imprints, 1794-1820," *Kentucky Historical Society Register* 42 (1944) 99-119.

MERKEL, BENJAMIN. *The Antislavery Controversy in Missouri, 1819-1865.* (Ph.D. diss., Washington University, 1939).

MICHAUX, F. A. *Travels to the West of the Alleghany Mountains.* London: Crosby, 1805.

MISSOURI, HOUSE OF REPRESENTATIVES. *Journal, First General Assembly, First Session.* St. Louis: Edward Charless, 1822.

MOTT, FRANK LUTHER. *Golden Multitudes, the Story of Best Sellers in the United States.* New York: Macmillan, 1947.

New Trade Directory for Philadelphia Anno 1800. Philadelphia: Way & Groff, 1799.

ORR, ISABEL. "The First Fifty Years of Printing in Missouri," (Unpub. M.S. thesis, Columbia University, 1937).

PERRIN, WILLIAM HENRY. *The Pioneer Press of Kentucky.* Louisville: Morton, 1888.

"Records of Pennsylvania Marriages, Prior to 1810," *Pennsylvania Archives*, 2d Ser., v. 9. Harrisburg: Hart, 1880.

RUMBALL-PETRE, EDWIN A. R. *America's First Bibles.* Portland, Maine: Southworth-Anthoensen Press, 1940.

SCHARF, JOHN T. *History of St. Louis City and County.* Philadelphia: Everts, 1883. 2 vols.

SHEPARD, ELIHU. *Autobiography.* St. Louis: George Knapp, 1869.

STANSBURY, ARTHUR J. *Report of the Trial of James H. Peck.* Boston: Hilliard, Gray & Co., 1833.

STAPLES, CHARLES R. *The History of Pioneer Lexington.* Lexington: Transylvania Press, 1939.

STEVENS, WALTER B. *St. Louis; the Fourth City, 1764-1911.* St. Louis: Clarke, 1911. 2 vols.

SUTTON, WALTER. *The Western Book Trade: Cincinnati as a Nineteenth-Century Publishing and Book-Trade Center.* Columbus: Ohio State University Press, 1961.

THOMAS, ISAIAH. *History of Printing in America.* Albany: Munsell, 1874. 2 vols.

U. S. DEPT. OF STATE. *The Territorial Papers of the United States.* Washington: Government Printing Office, 1934-1960. 25 vols.

U. S. *Statutes at Large.* Boston: Little & Brown, 1846.

VAN RAVENSWAAY, CHARLES. "Pioneer Presses in Missouri," *Missouri Historical Society Bulletin* 7 (1951) 296-301.

VIOLETTE, EUGENE M. "Spanish Land Claims in Missouri," *Washington University Studies* 8 (1921) Humanistic Series, No. 2, 167-200.

WALL, THOMAS. *The Sign of Doctor Hay's Head.* Dublin: M. H. Gill, 1958.

WROTH, LAWRENCE. *Parson Weems.* Baltimore: Eichelberger, 1911.

INDEX

158